A Rough Road

Patrick J. Bird

Dedicated to:
Mom and Pop

CONTENTS

AUTHOR'S PREFACE

At age four, which was a long time ago, I contracted polio and underwent nineteen months of "reconstruction." This is the story of those months told as carefully and truthfully as possible.

The events and timelines portrayed here are factual. The New York State Reconstruction Home, the main setting for the narrative, is now the Helen Hayes Hospital, West Haverstraw, N.Y. Descriptions of the facility as it appeared in the early 1940's are based upon historical documents provided by staff at the Helen Hayes Hospital. The orthopedic and rehabilitation techniques portrayed are accurate representations of the art and science of polio treatment in the United States in the early 1940's as I understand it from my research.

Portrayals of family members and relatives are true to life, as they appeared to me. Depictions of others (nurses, doctors, and staff, as well as "best friend Joey") are composites drawn from memory fragments dating back seventy years and elaborated on for the sake of the story.

The dialogue is invented, of course. My recollection of conversations from yesterday is difficult; never mind recollections from early childhood. Nevertheless, the dialects, word usage, and tone of family members and relatives, as well as the sentiments they express in the narrative, are reasonably accurate based upon my intimate knowledge of these wonderful people. Except for family members, the names of other characters were changed for the sake of privacy.

Nothing in this publication is intended to ridicule or belittle any of the medical professionals or staff members employed by New York State Reconstruction Home at the time of this story. The sometimes negative, angry, or disparaging words attributed to some is intended to reflect the frustration, bewilderment, and the panic experienced by the protagonist, Paddy, and his parents, Bill and Nan. To the best of my knowledge, the care Paddy received was based upon the best scientific knowledge of the day and was delivered by well-trained and well-meaning professionals.

This book has been written first of all to be a good read about a four-year-old child who is placed in a sterile, alien environment where, for over a year and one-half, he must cope with a series of harsh physical and psychological challenges. The story should appeal to anyone who has experienced long-term separation from home and family, at whatever age or for whatever reason. It is also a glimpse into the treatment of polio victims in the early 1940's, prior to World War II.

In one way, this publication could not be timelier. Over one million people in the United States are survivors of the polio epidemics, making polio the second largest disability behind stroke. Paddy's story could spark bittersweet memories for many of these individuals (most are over sixty-five) as they reminisce about their "reconstruction."

ACKNOWLEDGEMENTS

Music and lyrics for "Across the Alley from the Alamo" were composed by Joe Greene (1915-1986). The *Columbo* verses cited are an imprecise version, recalled from my childhood, of a bawdy poem by *T. S. Eliot* (1888-1985). The variation on the traditional old English rhyme *Thirty Days Hath September* and the ditty *Mama, Mama Take Me Home* are childhood remembrances as well, to which I am unable to attribute an author. The *Shm-ha-in* ghost story is built on a Celtic folk tale, again as remembered from childhood. Its author, too, is unknown to me and perhaps unknowable.

A key source for historical aspects of this book is David M. Oshinsky's Pulitzer Prize winning history, *Polio: An American Story (New York: Oxford Press, 2005)*.

I wish to thank Ms. Mary Creagh, Director of Public Affairs at Helen Hayes Hospital, for her hospitality and for providing me with access to historical documents housed at the facility. In addition, I am indebted to my wife Mary Newell and to Katherine Boyle for reviewing this manuscript and providing invaluable comments, editorial suggestions, and above all encouragement.

After contracting polio in 1940, four-year-old Paddy spends nineteen months in a "reconstruction home" far from home and family. This is his story of that time. It is not, however, "a pity the polio kid saga," although aching sadness and loneliness, the pain and disappoints of rehabilitation, as well as adult insensitivity and meanness are critical to this deeply personal narrative. It is a tale about the resilient spirit common to all children.

With warmth and humor, it tells about Paddy's caregivers, who in their individual ways serve as stand-in parents, and about his many adventures and misadventures during his long months of "reconstruction," including his enlightening friendship with a mischievous youngster suffering from spina bifida.

Also woven into the story are relevant aspects of the polio epidemics during the early 1940's:

- The mysterious summer infantile paralysis (polio) scourges are nearing its peak in the United States. Efforts to control the virus have closed parks, beaches, swimming pools, and movie houses while school doors remain locked until the epidemic passes.

- Treatment of those infected with the paralytic form of the disease is still rudimentary, including immobilizing limbs in casts and splints (in an attempt to prevent disfigurement) and full body encasement in the dreaded iron lung for those contracting the bulbar form of the disease, which attacks the nerves controlling breathing and swallowing.

· Painkillers, to help relieve the terrible muscle cramps, are discouraged by doctors fearing the drugs might cause further harm to the already besieged nervous system. Quinine is preferred but largely ineffective.

· Rehabilitation consists primarily of prolonged rest, the passive manipulation of paralyzed muscles, and corrective surgery that is often unwise. Methods that are more effective await the innovations of Sister Kenny and the knowledge to be gained treating wounded World War II soldiers.

· Polio survivors in wheelchairs, vaulting along on crutches, or tottering about on withered limbs are often stigmatized: *feeble and likely retarded.* Even President Roosevelt, stricken with polio in the summer of 1921, goes to great lengths to hide his atrophied legs from the public.

· The Salk Polio Vaccine is still ten years in the future.

Essential to the tale are Paddy's immigrant parents, Bill and Nan—a match not necessarily made in Heaven. In the telling black and white wedding photograph that hung prominently on their living room wall, Bill is standing slightly behind Nan, his left hand placed tentatively on her arm. He looks dapper in a snugly tailored suit, vest, striped tie, lapel carnation, and handkerchief neatly folded in his jacket pocket. His mouth is tight as his eyes stare off into the distance, as if seeing an uncertain future. Nan smiles from under a large brimmed hat tilted back on her head. She, too, is quite fashionable in a sleek white flapper-style gown, matching lace bodice affixed with a bouquet, fingerless gloves extending to her elbows, and a silk sash tied loosely around her waist. Scrolled neatly at the bottom right corner of the wedding picture is *June 1932.*

At the time the picture was taken, Bill was thirty-three years old and employed as an elevator operator and houseboy at the New York City Yale Club. Nan, then twenty-four, was a maid at the Mayflower Hotel across town. They had met two years earlier at the Irish dances held in the then famous and raucous Greenwich Village Rialto Ballroom. That was just days after Bill, a British merchant seaman, *jumped ship* and strolled leisurely from Manhattan's Pier 54 with his kit slung over his shoulder, and Nan, an Irish immigrant, stepped ashore at Ellis Island clutching a canvas satchel holding all she had in the world.

Bill was born in 1899 in Liverpool, England, the eleventh of nineteen siblings. The family lived well until his seventh year, when his father, a hard drinking Scotsman, lost his milk distributing business *betting the ponies.* After that, life was tough. "It was first up best dressed," Bill would laugh telling the story. In spite of the family misfortune, Bill completed twelfth grade, a good education for the time. He then joined the British Army, serving four years in India. This was followed by ten years in the British Merchant Service, stoking the coal-fired furnaces that powered ships of the day.

Elbow on the bar, a whisky and beer in easy reach, he loved to recount, in snappy Liverpool *scouse* (a blend of the Northern England dialect and Irish brogue), his "years serv'n the Crown":

Ay was stationed near the Khyber Pass, in Peshawar—a lance corporal with a team of six hoses and a 76 mm field gun in me charge. Every now and then, we'd parade with the gun—me, in princely style, ride'n the lead 'ores. But regimental prizefighter, that was me real job—train'n each day with a fight every few weeks, often in Delhi, sometimes even Bombay. Ay was Bantamweight Champion of the British Expeditionary Force in India me second year, ay was. After that, it was all gravy. Even 'ad an Indian lad to clean me clothes, shine me boots, and shave me smooth as a baby's arse—before ay even woke up me in the morn'n. Ah! I'll tell you, a lovely life the army was, blewdy wonderful!

Now the sea—that was a different kettle-o'-fish. Shovel'n coal and push'n a wheelbarrow of coal and red-hot ash—four hours on and four hours off—in boiler room temperatures of 130 degrees or more. And between shifts, fight'n all comers for a few quid— as there was no weight class at sea. It was an 'ard life. 'Ad some fine times, though. But that day ay walked off me last ship—*The City of Lancaster* was her name—ay never even took a glance back at 'er. America! The greatest country in the world it is, and ay seen 'em all.

Nan, nine years younger than Bill, was middle child among four brothers and three sisters. She entered the world in 1907, her home a thatched roof cottage perched on nineteen hilly acres in County Mayo, Ireland. *The Farm*, as she called it, was more rock than soil, scarcely able to sustain the brood. So, as each of the children came of age, they were expected to *find their own way*—except for the oldest son who by Irish tradition inherited the land. *Their own way* typically meant menial work, marriage, *the sacred callin'*, or more often than not—*'tis aff to America.*

With little more than a fourth grade education Nan was the first in her family to immigrate. In her soft, lyrical tones of the West of Ireland, she would tell longingly of that last night before *catchin' the ship at Cobh:*

Everyone came, each contributin' a dish or drink as best they could. The cottage was packed—packed to overflow. An' the music! Oh! It was nonstop, it was. Jimmy Burns fiddlin' away. Malcolm, his brother, playin' the tin whistle. An' Corey O'Conner beatin' away at the Celtic drum—had a crush on Corey, I did. An' us all singin' an' dancin' through the night.

Even father—a strappin' six-foot an' teetotaler by nature—had more than a sniff-av-the-cork, God love him. An' poor Mother, there she was smilin' an' rushin' about to be sure all had their fill. But she wasn't happy, not at all. Sure, I could tell. 'Mother,' I said as I took her aside, 'you don't want to be worrin' yerself about me. I'll be back before you know it with a rich Yank on me arm—yer'ill see'.

She took me hand to her soft cheek, her eyes swollen with tears, an' kissed it. 'Oh, Lord willin' darlin',' she sighed, 'an' wouldn't that be just gran'— gran' indeed. She knew though, as did I, I was gone— gone for good. An' as for the rich Yank—Jaysus forgive me—didn't I come up with an Englishman.

Sweet are the uses of adversity,
Which, like the toad, ugly and venomous,
Wears yet a precious jewel in his head...

William Shakespeare
As You Like It

CHAPTER I

A Fall and a Bump
September 24, 1940
Day: One

"'Tis wicked, Margaret. It killin' an' cripplin' all those paur children, God love 'em. But closin' the pools an' parks—leavin' them with nothin' to do. Not even the movies. I don't know."

Paddy peddles his tricycle into the apartment house courtyard and circles around his mom and Aunt Margaret, standing watching him.

"Ooo, Nan, sure, they must. 'Tis all the filth—'tis that that causes it. Just yesterday, didn't Sadie McCoy tell me how when she was a child the police went around shootin' stray cats an' dogs an' the firemen washed down the streets every day with tons of water?"

Paddy continues on to the top of the courtyard. Seeing the brass numerals *6830* above the doorway, he stops and completes the address in his mind: *Burns Street, Forrest Hills, Long Island, New York.* He just learned it from his mom after being lost in Coney Island. He then gazes up to the top floor proudly thinking: *It's a really big building and my pop is the super.*

"Blessed little good it did, I'm sure," Nan says. "An' the *authorities*, so they call themselves, sayin' one thing then another. An' us goin' mad worrin' over every sniffle."

Turning around, Paddy peddles back down the courtyard past his mom and Aunt Margaret.

"Oh, indeed, Nan, indeed, still..."

Reaching the sidewalk, he looks back, raising one hand from the handlebars, and waves at them.

"Watch where your goin' darlin'!" his mom calls out, interrupting her sister.

The tricycle wobbles. Paddy reaches frantically for the handlebar—too late. The front wheel bounces off the curb and tumbles him into the street.

"You all right, Paddy?"

He opens his eyes surprised to see his mom kneeling beside him with Aunt Margaret standing behind her, looking a little fuzzy to him.

"I don't feel good, Mommy. My head hurts," he whimpers, tears rolling down his cheeks.

"Let's have a look." She takes his chin and gently turns his head. "Appears yer'ill have a bit of av a lump. Ah well, life's full of hard knocks. Yer'ill live."

Kissing the mounting lump above his ear, she wipes his tears away with the back of her hand.

"Come now," she smiles, "let's go inside. I said you could ride for fifteen minutes. Times up, besides 'tis gettin' cold."

Nan helps her son to his feet, takes his hand, and they walk toward the apartment house entrance, Aunt Margaret behind them carrying the tricycle grousing, "You must be more careful with this 'ting or yer'ill be breakin' yer neck."

* * *

Lying on the couch beneath a blanket and a pillow under his head, Paddy holds ice wrapped in a towel to the bump while daydreaming about walking to the railroad tracks that morning with Pop and *the girls*. The tracks are across a field by the tennis stadium. They waited there a long time until the train came—fast and loud, shaking the ground. As it flew by, they waved, laughed, and sang their song about the Navajo and his pony that went walking along the railroad tracks: *and wish-n' not a look-in—toot! toot!—they never came back!* He then picked flowers, blue and yellow ones, for Mom who had *the nerves* and stayed home.

Across the room from Paddy sitting cross-legged on the floor, *the girls* are listening to *Mister Keen, Tracer of Lost Persons!* It's just starting. *The girls* are Kate, his sister. She's seven. Patsy, she's four, same age as Paddy. And there's Betty who is three.

Patsy and Betty are cousins living with them now in the small apartment. Their mom, Aunt Elizabeth, died last winter along with the child she was carrying. Soon after, her husband died as well. *'It was a broken heart that did it,* Nan claims. That was Uncle Pat, Paddy's namesake,

"Well, I'll be aff," Aunt Margaret says to her sister, who is moving a chair for herself up to the radio. "'Gettin' dark, it is. Wouldn't want to be accosted by some big Negro on me way to the subway."

Aunt Margaret comes every Sunday for dinner. She is unmarried—*too full av religion to get a man,* Nan jokes to Margaret's chagrin—and lives in Astoria at Rivercrest Sanitarium where she's a housekeeper.

"Accosted by some big Negro," Nan answers, turning the sound up on the radio. "Sure, you should be so fortunate, Margaret."

"Nan! For God's sake! What an awful thing to say—an' in front of the children!"

Nan doesn't respond.

Taking her purse from the dining room table, Aunt Margaret comes over to Paddy.

"Now," she kisses his forehead, "you don't want to be forgettin' your prays tonight. With the help of the Lard, yer'ill be rite as rain in the mornin'."

"Okay." He smiles and kisses her cheek.

"Bye, darlin's," Aunt Margaret calls to the girls and walks to the door.

"Bye," they singsong, not looking from the radio.

Bill appears from the kitchen sipping a glass of beer. "So long, Margaret. Watch you don't get *accosted*." He laughs.

"An' sure—an' the likes of you would care?" She glances meanly at him.

Paddy closes his eyes and is soon into a dream:

The lifeguard lowers him from the tall chair into his mom's arms.
Holding him tight, all soft and warm, she runs up the beach,
zigzagging in and out, in and out of the surf.
Pop and the girls run ahead—zigzagging, zigzagging.
'Come on, Nan' his pop calls out, pointing to a massive black cloud rolling in if from the ocean.
'Hurry—let 'im run on his own—quickly now!'
She puts him down, the sand cold and wet.
'Run, Paddy—run fast,' she shouts as she races off zigzagging in and out, in and out, of the surf.
Shivering, shivering all over—the the icy rain drops stinging him—
he struggles to follow her.
He can't move.
He's sinking, sinking!
The sand sucking him under,
Squeezing his legs—crushing them!
He screams!

* * *

"Was soon after supper that he fell from the bike, Dr. Kline."

Paddy hears his mom's voice and opens his eyes. Dr. Kline is sitting beside him looking up at his parents standing together at the end of the couch, his pop smoking a cigarette.

"Then, about ten o'clock, with the girls aff to bed, he woke up crying something awful—his little leg muscles pulled tight as fiddle strings. Then the crampin', 'tis in his neck and back as well. And he's burning up with fever."

"Aye," his pop adds. "Breath'n hard, as well—try'n to get a breath."

"God love 'im," Nan heaves a sigh, "he's been in terrible pain, doctor."

"How long has he been asleep?"

Dr. Kline's craggy face turns to Paddy. Looking over the top of glasses, perched on the end of his nose, he feels the boy's head.

"A good hour now," she answers. "I rubbed his legs. After a while the cramps went away. An' he then fell back to sleep."

"Ah, you're awake." Dr. Kline gently presses what is now a walnut size bump. "How are you feeling, Paddy?"

"Okay," he whimpers, twisting his head from the doctor's hand.

"Well, let's take a look at you." The doctor stands with a grunt.

While Paddy watches anxiously, Dr. Kline removes his blanket, opens his pajama top, and taps his chest, making a light drumming sound. He then places a black satchel on the coach, opens it, takes out a stethoscope, and listens to the quick thumping of the little heart. Returning the stethoscope to the satchel, the doctor retrieves a pencil light and lowers his craggy face toward Paddy.

"Open your mouth," he whispers with whisky breath.

Paddy does as he is told, looking at the tangle of hairs twisting out of the doctor's giant nose.

Dr. Kline quickly examines his throat and ears. Next, he squeezes his legs all over, rolls him on his side, and pulls his pajama bottoms down.

Paddy tenses, feeling the thermometer enter him.

"Temperature is a little high still." Dr. Kline turns to Nan and Bill, letting Paddy roll back over. "Best we get him to Bellevue Hospital, though—if only as a precaution."

"Lard-help-us," Nan groans, making the *Sign-of-the-Cross*.

Dr. Kline then takes a small bottle and a big needle from the satchel, Paddy gazing intently at him, his heart racing. The doctor pushes the needle into the bottle, pulls it out, and points the tip straight up, letting drops of liquid trickle down the shaft.

"This will sting, young fellow—just a little," he says, rolling Paddy again on to his side.

"Ouch!" Paddy yelps.

"That's it—you're a brave boy." Dr. Kline pats the boy's behind, turns him back over, and pulls up the pajama bottoms.

"The shot will put him to sleep." He then looks to Nan and Bill while placing the needle and bottle back in the black satchel.

Dr. Kline stands, and he and his pop walk to the apartment door while his mom steps over and straightens his covers.

"Sure, darlin'," she says softly to him, "that wasn't half bad now, was it?"

He looks at her sorrowfully. "I'm going to the hospital?"

"We'll see. We'll see. Close your eyes now. Sleep now."

* * *

Bill in shirtsleeves and Dr. Kline in an overcoat and wearing a fedora stroll from the apartment building toward the doctor's car.

"Think it's polio?" Bill asks.

"He has the symptoms—but perhaps not. We'll have to wait and see."

"Maybe 'e got it at Coney Island?"

"When was that?"

"Week-ago-Friday."

"Could be, if indeed it is polio. Symptoms often begin seven to fourteen days after being infected. You know where Bellevue Hospital is located?"

"O' aye, Manhattan—First Avenue, downtown."

Dr. Kline nods in agreement. "And Nan, how is she?"

"The missus," Bill shakes his head, "sound as a pound all summer, but the nerves are act'n up again."

"Oh, how so?"

"Walk'n, mainly, and the constipation. She shakes, too. Can hardly thread a needle sometimes. Cigarette?"

"Thank you."

Bill pulls a pack of Chesterfields from his shirt pocket. The two men pause, light up, and continue toward the car.

"That's the damnable nature of multiple sclerosis," Dr. Kline says. "Good times lasting weeks, even months, then a relapse. Has she been seeing the neurologist, Dr. Colson?"

"Nah! She won't go. Says it's a waste a money."

"She should, you know."

"O' aye, but she's stubborn as a mule."

After continuing in silence for a few paces, Bill says, "Ay still don't understand it. She was fine when we married. Then it came on."

"Yes," Dr. Kline sighs, "no one seems to know the cause of *MS*. I was taught that a toxin or poison somehow infects the brain. Today, that notion is questioned. They say now it's a disruption of information going to and from the brain."

Shaking hands at the car, Bill says with a smile, "I appreciate ya come'n, it be'n Sunday, so late and all."

"I'll call Bellevue," Dr. Kline responds with a friendly nod. "Probably will be some time before an ambulance arrives."

Bill nods. "Thank you, doctor."

Heading back to the apartment house, Bill's thoughts turn from polio and MS to the pint of Four Roses whisky stashed in his basement workshop. His pace quickens.

* * *

The stretcher bumps at the rear of the ambulance and stops. Paddy lifts his head. Down the sidewalk, he sees the girls standing in their nightgowns and jackets hugging their chests. The sun is just rising behind them painting the scattered clouds pink.

Kate gives a little wave.

A man in a white jacket opens the ambulance door.

Paddy's head flops back.

His mom bends over him, her eyes red and swollen, and kisses his forehead, saying, "Your dad an' I will be along soon."

"I'll be okay, Mom," he whispers in her ear.

The men in white jackets move him feet first into the ambulance. Stretching his head back, he sees his pop lighting his cigarette. The ambulance door bangs shut—it's dark, scary now. A man in the white jacket sits beside him smiling. The ambulance jerks forward. The siren blares. He shrieks as the terrible cramps return.

CHAPTER II

It's Polio
September 25, 1940
Day: Two

Bill and Nan stand across the receiving counter from a thick-bodied nurse checking a ledger.

"Yeah. We got 'im," her hard-edged voice affirms. "I'll let the doctor know ya here."

"How long will it be?" Nan asks.

"Don't know. Ya not the only one here, ya know. Sit down. Wait ya turn."

"Eejit!" Nan mutters as they turn away to find a seat.

Settling into chairs in the back of the packed waiting area, Nan dozes off while Bill keeps a sharp eye on the admitting nurse, listening intently to her intermittent barking of names over the loudspeaker.

Nan soon jerks awake, poking him with her elbow.

"What?" he asks.

"Go ask that Nurse Nasty where the doctor's at."

"Nan, be patient, will you?"

"Sure, we've been patient an hour now, long enough."

"Been but fifteen minutes."

"Go on. Ask her." Nan pokes him again. "She won't bite you—at least yer'd suppose she won't."

"Ah, well." Bill rises from his chair.

At the receiving counter, Nurse Nasty is berating an old man in a beret.

"Ya wife's not here, Mr. Schwartz, must-a-took her somewhere else."

"They brought her in last night. I'm sure. Please, look again, if you would."

Moving her thick face over the counter toward the old man, she sneers. "She's! Not! Here!"

Mr. Schwartz totters off.

"My son, Paddy, e' is…" Bill addresses Nurse Nasty.

"I know! Wait ya turn like everyone else."

"Well?" Nan asks as Bill drops into his chair.

"Won't be too long now."

"*Too long?* An' how long is that?"

"Christ, Nan, not long!"

"Sure, there's no need to be takin' the Lard's name in vain," she says with another elbow jab.

Bill continues his worried surveillance while Nan drops her chin and dozes off again.

* * *

Two hours pass before Nurse Nasty's voice explodes over the loudspeaker calling their names.

"Let's go, Nan. That's us." Bill springs from his chair.

"What?" She jerks awake.

"It's our turn. Let's go before someone else is called," Bill says, helping her to her feet.

A tall redheaded doctor is flipping through pages on a clipboard at the receiving counter and looks up as they approach.

"Paddy's parents?"

"Aye, I'm his father. This is me little lady, Nan."

"My name is Doctor McMahan." The doctor places the clipboard on the counter. "Will you please follow me?"

"'Tis McMahon? That's what he said, wasn't it?" Nan says, clutching Bill's arm as they rush to keep pace with the doctor. "Sure, it's a gran' sign, Bill. An' doesn't he look for all the world like me father—Lord rest his soul—the red head an' all?"

"O aye. Spit'n image," Bill grumbles, having never set eyes on the man.

Dr. McMahon leads them from the elevator, down a long hallway, and into a small office crammed with cabinets and overflowing bookshelves. He slides behind a desk with a single blue folder on top. Behind him framed documents fill the wall. To their right, a window looks out on the East River—the Queensboro Bridge off in the distance, the sky gray.

"Please, have a seat." Dr. McMahon gestures toward two steel chairs in front of a desk.

"How's Paddy?" Nan asks nervously as they sit down.

Dr. McMahon opens the blue folder, studies it for a moment, and looks up at them. "I'm very sorry to tell you this," he says quietly. "Your boy does have polio."

"Saints preserve us." Nan drops her head making a quick *Sign- of- the Cross.*

"Ya sure?" Bill scoots forward in his chair.

"I'm afraid so. Still—well, we don't know how severe it is yet."

"An' the terrible cramps. What of them?" Nan asks.

"Paddy still gets them, but not as often now. He has been taking quinine sulfate and has had several short wave diathermy treatments, which has provided some relief."

"Short wave—how's that?" Bill asks.

"The muscle tissue is heated using high frequency oscillations of electrometric energy. It's a deep, penetrating heat that tends to decrease the spasms."

"Does it hurt him?" asks Nan.

"No, not at all."

"And the quinine?" Bill asks. "Thought that was for malaria."

"It's used mainly for that, but it also helps relieve severe cramping in some people."

Then, pushing the blue file aside, Dr. McMahon says, "I don't know what you know about the polio."

"Only what's in the papers," Bill replies.

"Well, let me try to explain." Dr. McMahon leans toward them folding his hands in front of him. "Our muscles are composed of bundles of thread-like fibers. Each of these fibers has the ability to shorten, to contract. When the fibers contract, they move our limbs and other parts of our bodies. And they work together in team fashion. For example, more fibers are set to work to lift a paperweight than, say, a pencil.

"Now, each tiny fiber is controlled by a nerve cell, which is located in the spinal column. These so-called motor neurons are essentially switches. They turn the muscle fiber on and off. When turned on, the fiber contracts. When turned off, the fiber relaxes. The spinal column is like a large switchboard. Okay, so far?"

Bill and Nan nod.

"Polio is caused by a virus that attacks and kills motor neurons, specifically those that control the muscle fibers in our limbs, trunk, and diaphragm. Other nerves that allow us to feel sensations, like hot and cold, for instance, are not affected by the poliovirus."

"And with Paddy?" Nan asks, tears filling the corners of her eyes.

"Appears to be his legs, mainly."

"The switches," Bill asks, "they'll work again when the virus goes away?"

"No." The doctor shakes his head sadly. "Once broken, the switch is broken for good. When enough of these switches are destroyed, the entire muscle can be severely weakened or paralyzed. Any resulting weakness or paralysis is permanent. Motor neurons do not regenerate, come back."

Nan buries her head in her hands choking back sobs.

"However, and this is important," Dr. McMahon goes on.

Nan looks up. Bill moves forward in his chair.

"In a damaged muscle, there may be healthy muscle fibers—their switches unaffected by the poliovirus—that can be trained to take over for those affected. Muscle fibers performing double duty, you might say. The function of a leg, for instance, although weakened is not totally lost."

Dr. McMahon pauses, looking at them with concern. He then adds, "One more thing..."

"There's more?" says Bill, taking a deep breath. Nan stares bleary-eyed at the doctor.

"Well, yes. Although, as I said, Paddy's legs seem to be the problem, his diaphragm muscle—the breathing muscle—may also have been weakened by the virus." The doctor pauses again, as if trying to avoid continuing. He goes on. "When this happens, a respirator, an iron lung, is used to assist breathing."

"Jaysus-Mary-an'-Joseph," Nan gasps. "Paddy—he's in an iron lung?"

"Yes, I'm afraid so. His breathing was labored when he was admitted. He was unable to even count to ten without taking a breath—one of the tests we use."

"Blewdy 'ell." Bill shakes his head.

"It's just a precaution." Dr. McMahon raises his hands in a reassuring motion. "Evaluating a child's respiratory status at this early stage is difficult. We'll know more in a few days."

"How's it work?" Bill asks.

"The respirator? Well, it's really quite simple. The whole body, except the head, fits into what is essentially a sealed cylinder and motors move air in and out of it. As the air is forced out, the pressure inside the chamber is reduced. This causes the chest to rise, pulling air through the child's nose and mouth to fill the lungs—like inhaling, taking a breath. When air is sucked back into the chamber, pressure inside increases, the chest falls, and the lungs are compressed, forcing air out. The child exhales, breathes out."

"Like a bellows?" Bill searches his pockets for a cigarette.

"Yes, a bellows," Dr. McMahon nods. "Now, I want to stress again, the iron lung is only a safeguard for Paddy. In most cases, the strength of the diaphragm muscle slowly but surely returns—perhaps in just days. As I said, we'll see."

"Can I smoke?"

"Sure." Dr. McMahon slides an ashtray across the desk.

"Like one?" Bill asks, tapping a Chesterfield from the pack.

"No thank you." The doctor eyes the cigarettes with a weak smile. "Trying to quit."

After a minute of quiet, Bill lighting up and Nan nervously wiping her face and hands with a handkerchief, Nan asks, "Can we visit Paddy now, doctor?"

"I'm sorry, we should wait a while—next week or so. After he is well beyond the acute phase."

"For a moment—no more."

Raising from his chair, prompting Nan and Bill to do the same, the doctor smiles, "Well, you can see him for a few minutes."

"God bless you," Nan says happily.

"I'll have a nurse take you to him." Dr. McMahon steps to the door. "But I must insist that it be a very brief visit. In the meantime, I'll set an appointment for us to meet again the week after next."

"Lard help us!" Nan turns abruptly to him. "We have three other children at home. Because of Paddy, will the darlin's get it as well?"

"Actually, they may already have been infected—as most children have."

"Oh, Lard save us," Nan gasps.

"No, no, don't worry." Dr. McMahon places an assuring hand on her shoulder. "They're probably all fine. The poliovirus causes paralysis, or true polio, in no more than ten percent of those infected. In most cases, our immune systems fight it off. Some people feel nothing. Others just get flu-like symptoms, fever, headache, sore throat—and recover in a day or so."

"Thank God." Nan sighs.

"Still," Dr. McMahon adds, "you must keep your eye on them. Contact Dr. Kline right away if you suspect a problem—flu-like symptoms."

Bill shakes the doctor's hand. "We'll keep a sharp eye 'em. Thanks."

Smiling cheerily, Nan says, "McMahon! A fine Irish name you have. Thank you." She takes his hand. "And may the Lard's blessin's be forever with you."

* * *

They are led down a series of corridors, Nan holding tight to Bill's arm, and finally stop before large double doors.

"Please put these on," the nurse says, handing them each a surgical mask.

She then swings the door open, steps aside, and invites them to enter. Crossing the threshold, they freeze.

"Jaysus, Bill." Nan's fingernails dig into his arm.

"I'll be damned," Bill groans.

Filling a depressingly bright gymnasium-size room is row after row of shiny steel cylinders, each sprouting the head of a child.

"Lard, Lard—silver caskets at Heaven's Gate." Nan begins to weep. "The paur, paur, darlin's."

"Buck-up, Nan," says Bill, pulling in a deep breath.

They trail the nurse down the center row of cylinders. The smell is strong, hospital and machine oil. Dark, sleepy eyes follow them as they pass one disembodied child after another. Inside the cylinder portholes, little chests can be seen rising and falling. It's quiet, just the rush of air escaping the iron lungs—*whoosh-whoosh-whoosh.*

CHAPTER III

Dr. McMahon's Recommendation
October 4, 1940
Day: Eleven

"We was 'ere ten days ago," Bill says firmly to Nurse Nasty. "Dr. McMahon, he made the appointment for today, two o'clock,"

"Noth'n here. Maybe it's for tomorrow," she grumbles, looking over a chart. "I'll call. Take a seat."

"We'll wait right here," Nan says sharply. "If you look, yer'ill see the clock right there behind you says it's almost two. We'll not be late."

With a spiteful smile, Nurse Nasty picks up the phone, dials, listens, says their names, listens again, and hangs up.

"Ya can go up. Elevator to the third floor." She points without looking toward the bank of elevators off to her left.

"Sure, think we don't know our way." Nan turns sharply from the receiving desk taking Bill's arm.

Dr. McMahon stands as Nan and Bill enter through the doorway. ""Come in. Come in. Have a seat. I've some good news."

"Paddy's better?" Nan asks cautiously.

"Yes, much better. His breathing has normalized, and, I am pleased to say, he's no longer on the respirator."

"Oh, thank God," Nan says, as she and Bill sit down.

"His legs, however, are no better. He still has occasional fits of severe cramping. And we don't know just how much damage the virus had done to the muscles."

"When will you know that?" Nan asks.

"It's difficult to say—several months."

"Months?" Bill asks, with a surprised glance at his wife.

"Yes, perhaps. What is certain is that he will need continued hospital care, and for some time."

"He'll be staying here then?" Nan asks.

"No, what I recommend is that we transfer him to the New York State Reconstruction Home."

"New York State Reconstruction Home?" asks Bill.

"Yes. It's a lovely place on sixty acres situated above the Hudson River. A relatively small facility—eighty children or so in residence. About one quarter with polio. Others have a range of problems—osteomyelitis, tuberculosis, and an assortment of physical defects and deformities."

"Defects and deformities. An' what would they be?" Nan looks uneasily from the doctor to Bill.

"Clubfoot, spina bifida, scoliosis and things of that nature. Although the children are older than Paddy, Dr. Strasburg has agreed to accommodate him. I know Dr. Strasburg well. I did part of my residency there. That was a few years ago. It was then called the Hospital for the Care of Crippled and Deformed Children."

"Crippled an' deformed children—dear God." Nan gasps.

"Yes, an unfortunate name—why it was changed." Dr. McMahon nods, regretting he mentioned the old name.

"Where's it at?" Bill asks.

"West Haverstraw. About forty miles north, toward Albany, off Route 9W."

"Forty miles, that's a long way, and we've no car."

"Yes, well, I understand. There is a train from Grand Central Station to West Haverstraw. And that is the best place for your son right now. There, we will get a better reading on his condition and he can begin rehabilitation."

A hard splattering of rain suddenly slaps the windowpane, drawing all eyes to the outside.

"Miserable weather. Won't let up." Bill addresses no one in particular. Then looking at the doctor, he asks, "When will he be sent to—what's it?"

"The New York State Reconstruction Home—a day or two."

CHAPTER IV

The N.Y.S. Reconstruction Home
October 11, 1940
Day: Eighteen

"Would you believe the place, Bill," Nan grumbles, walking around the room. "Dreary lookin' brick walls, bare pipes strung across the ceilin', an' the radiator hangin' there up on the wall hissin' away. Should be fixed an' on the floor where it belongs. An' not a stitch of cloth on the window. Like some ol' basement storage room, it is."

"Aye," says Bill, eying the silver painted radiator. "The valve needs to be unplugged, perhaps tightened some."

He then turns to Paddy. "And how was the ride up, son?"

"It was fun, but they didn't turn on the siren, and..."

"Let him tell you all about it a little later, Bill," Nan interrupts Paddy. "We must go now and see the doctor."

"But you just got here," Paddy protests, as his mom comes over to the bed and kisses his cheek.

"We'll be back by before we leave ter say goodbye."

Paddy watches them leave. Then, sitting up high against the back of his bed, his eyes wander around the room taking in his new surroundings for the first time.

Next to his bed, he has his own nightstand. The hissing radiator hangs above it. Past the radiator is the window with a large tree just outside. Then, another nightstand next to a second bed, which has no covers, only a gray mattress and gray pillow.

At the end of the empty bed, in the corner, is a sink. Two chairs sit by it. They're like ones at home in the kitchen, but green not blue. Directly across from the foot of his bed is the door. It's open. He can see across the hallway where there's a window. Outside is a field with trees.

Paddy slides down under the covers, thinking: *It's not so bad like Mom says.*

A then nurse walks into the room. "Hello, there." She smiles.

"Hi."

"You just arrived, I understand."

"The ambulance brought me."

"Well, welcome, Paddy."

She comes over beside him. Her hair is red, fuzzy-like, and tied in back with a green ribbon. A nurse hat looking like a sailboat rests on her head.

"My name is Nurse Kelly. I'll be in an' out most of the day to take care of you." She picks a comic book up from beside him on the bed. "Oh, an' what have we here?"

"It's the new *Red Ryder*. Pop got it for me from Mr. Harmon. He lives in our apartment building on the top floor—does Red Ryder for the comic book, the funny pages, too."

She looks at the cover. "And this must be Red Ryder himself standing here with that big gun on his shoulder?"

"Yes. And that's Thunder, his horse, behind him." He smiles. "You know, you talk kind-a like my mom."

"Do I now?" She places the comic back beside Paddy. "Is she from Ireland?"

"Uh-huh. Aunt Margaret, too."

"That's gran'." Nurse Kelly tucks in his covers. "Now, you should nap some until your parents return. You look a bit tuckered out."

* * *

"Paddy." He opens his eyes.

A nurse is leaning over him. Not Nurse Kelly. This one has short, curly white hair, a wrinkly face, and eyeglasses on the end of her nose, like Dr. Kline.

"Hello, my name is Nurse Edelstein," she says.

"Hi. My mom and pop back?" He sits up looking past her.

"They were here and left. They didn't want to wake you. You have been sleeping quite a while. Now, have some dinner before it gets cold."

"They didn't give me a kiss goodbye."

"They said to tell you they had to catch the train home."

She then takes a tray of food from his nightstand and places it on his lap. He glances around the room again, suddenly feeling sad: *It's like an old basement storage room just like Mom said.*

"I don't like it here," he sobs, pushing the tray away. Tears fill his eyes. "And they—they just left me here."

"Come now, you'll see them again soon. Have your dinner."

"No! I don't want it!" He shoves the tray hard.

"I'll have none of that, young man!" Nurse Edelstein quickly stops the tray from sliding off the bed. "If you don't want the food, fine, but don't be fresh!"

She returns the tray to his nightstand. Paddy lies down, rolling on his side away from her. Shutting his teary eyes, he falls back to sleep, dreaming:

> Sitting on a stick gripping the ends,
> He pulls up, lifting the stick against his bottom.
> He rises, floating above his bed, then glides around the room, out the window.
> Up, up, into the sky he soars—tingling all over with delight.
> Far below, he sees his apartment house, the tennis stadium, the big field, the railroad tracks.
> Pop, the girls, Aunt Margaret, and Mom, too, are there, all looking down he tracks, waiting.
> He lets up on the stick.
> Gliding down.
> His mom looks up.
> She waves, calling—hurry! Hurry!
> He flies faster.
> His heart racing now, pounding his chest.
> The train comes—rushes by.
> They are all singing:
>> Across the alley the Alamo,
>> Lived a pinto pony and a Navajo...
> Suddenly—he's flying up! Up!
> He stops pulling up on the stick.
> But it won't let him go down!
> Just up! Up! Soaring higher! Higher!
> His mom is getting smaller, smaller.
> She's tiny—a dot—she's gone!
> They're all gone!
> Mom-my! Mom-my!

He screeches awake, his legs rigid—as if each muscle is competing with another to snap his bones.

"Here, child, drink this, quinine, will help stop the cramps," says Nurse Edelstein, appearing beside his bed raising his head.

He gulps down the bitter liquid, clawing at his covers and moaning with pain.

CHAPTER V

Immobilization
October 14, 1940
Day: Twenty-one

"Do you know the nurse that was here last night?"

"Nurse Edelstein—yes, a bit," answers Nurse Kelly.

"She doesn't like me."

"Sure, what makes you think that?"

"She just doesn't."

"You done?"

"Yes."

"Take hold, as I showed you."

Paddy wraps his arms around her neck and pulls himself up from the bed pan. She wipes him and slides the bedpan out, and he lowers himself to the mattress.

"She was mean to me."

Nurse Kelly wrinkles her nose, covers the bedpan with a towel and places it on nightstand by the empty bed.

"Nurse Edelstein can be a grouch, so I'm told. Best to stay on her good side."

"You ever been to Coney Island?" Paddy asks, while Nurse Kelly helps him into a fresh gown.

"Sure, who hasn't?"

"I got lost there last summer, in Coney Island."

"Ooh, that must av been scary?"

"Yeah, but was fun, scary fun. The lifeguard found me, carried me way up on his tall chair. And he lifted me over his head and turned me around and around, blowing his whistle real loud. I could see the Parachute ride, way far away. The Wonder Wheel. The Cyclone— that's where everyone screams. And the ice cream store up on the boardwalk. Pop takes us there. The cotton candy stand next to it. Then jillions and jillions of people all down the beach. And the big, flat ocean--goes all the way to Ireland, Mom says."

"It does indeed, and 'tis a very long way," Nurse Kelly sighs, fluffing his pillow and straightening the covers.

"Mom came and got me from the lifeguard. Then it started raining real hard so we had to go home. And the train, it got stuck in the tunnel for a long time. The wheel fell off. That's what mom said and..."

There's a soft knock on the open door. They turn to see a man with a crooked-like walk coming into the room carrying a tray balanced on one hand over his head.

"Hi-o-kiddo. Bet ya as hungry as a two-bellied goat. Ya ate noth'n last night," he says, setting the food tray on the nightstand.

"Yes, thanks."

He smiles—showing no teeth on top, just gums— turns, and limps from the room.

"What's his name?" Paddy asks as Nurse Kelly places a low table over his legs and puts the tray on it.

"Mr. Martin."

"What's wrong with his legs?"

"Got polio as a boy, like you."

"Oh." Paddy nods, hungrily eyeing breakfast: oatmeal, brown sugar on top, a small bottle of milk, and a banana.

* * *

After breakfast, as Paddy watches squirrels outside the window, three of them running up and down the big tree, over and over again, a sound— *clip-clop, clip-clop*— comes from the hallway. He turns from the window as a gurney roll into the room—*clip-clop, clip-clop.*

Behind the gurney, ducking his head coming through the doorway, is a huge man in a white jacket. Paddy watches him thinking: *The Jack and the Beanstalk giant, but he's black, not green.*

The giant rolls the *clip-clopping* gurney up to the bed.

"Had ya breakfast, boy?" he asks in a deep voice, like the *Fat Man* on the radio.

"Yes." Paddy nods.

"Good—ya go'n for a ride."

"A ride?"

"Yup."

"Where to?"

Without answering, the giant turns down Paddy's covers, lifts him on to the gurney, places a pillow under his head, and covers him with a blanket.

Paddy looks up at him as they *clip-clop* from the room. "My name's Paddy."

"I know. I'm Johnny Cant," the giant answers, staring straight ahead.

"What's making the noise?"

"Wheel's broke," he grumbles.

"Oh, sounds like a horse walking."

"Yeah, a horse," he says with a chuckle, his *Fat Man* voice sounding a little friendlier.

They *clip-clop* down several hallways. The gurney then pushes through two silvery doors and into a bright room. In the middle of the room is a steel table with a large light hanging over it. Johnny Cant wheels Paddy to the table.

He quickly uncovers him, lifts him on to the cold, hard surface, and covers him again.

"Be back later," he says.

He then swings the gurney around and *clip-clops* out the silvery doors, ducking through the doorway.

Lifting his head, Paddy looks around the room—cabinets, a sink, a table and chair, and a cart near the door. Everything is white. No windows.

He lies back staring up at the big light. He listens, holding his breath. It's very quiet. Then lots of footsteps. As he turns his head to look, the big light suddenly pops on— painfully bright. He flings his arm over his eyes.

"Hello, Paddy. I'm Dr. Strasburg."

Paddy peeks out from under his arm. A man with a mustache—looking like a black caterpillar above his lips—is smiling down at him while moving the light from his eyes.

"Comfy?" asks a nurse standing next to the doctor. She has hair rising high up from her head: *Cotton candy, yellow cotton candy* goes through his mind.

"Yes, ma'am," he answers, taking his arm from his eyes.

"And how are we today?" Dr. Strasburg asks.

"Okay." Paddy slides up on his elbows turning from the cotton candy to the caterpillar.

"Good. That's Dr. Ingersoll." He points toward the end of the table. "He's an intern—a beginning doctor. He'll be assisting me."

Paddy looks and sees a blond man with a smiling face. Next to him, not smiling, is a woman in a blue apron.

"Hi, Paddy," Dr. Ingersoll waves cheerfully.

"That's Nurse Slaton beside Dr. Ingersoll. And here next to me is Nurse McCormick. Nurse McCormick and Nurse Slaton will be helping out as well."

"Helping do what?"

"Nothing bad. Now, let's see your legs."

"Lie down," Nurse McCormick orders.

Plopping back, Paddy feels his gown lifting.

"No!" he rises from the table, reaching quickly to push his gown down and cover his nakedness.

"Stay down!" Nurse McCormick says sharply.

"I want my mommy." Paddy flops back, tears filling his eyes.

"None of that," Nurse McCormick looks sharply at him, the sides of her mouth are turned down meanly. Then with a half-smile she adds, "You must be a bit more grown up here. You're not a big sissy, are you?"

"No, I'm not." He bites down on his lip as the tears escape.

"Have you had cramps lately, Paddy?" Dr. Strasburg asks, gently feeling his legs.

"Yes," he mutters.

"When?"

"Last night."

"Bad?"

"Uh-huh."

"Both legs?"

"That one most." He points blindly at his left leg.

"Okay." Dr. Strasburg turns briskly to Dr. Ingersoll. "Let's get started."

Paddy lifts his head.

"Down!" Nurse McCormick growls.

He slumps back.

"Dr. Ingersoll," Dr. Strasburg says quietly, "we will immobilize the legs in an abducted position. The feet flexed—like so."

Paddy feels his legs being spread apart and his left foot being pushed up as he watches the blue apron nurse walk away from the table.

"Immobilization prevents the non-affected muscles from pulling on the paralyzed ones, which could deform the legs. That's a particular danger in children with their bones still growing. You were taught all this in medical school, I'm sure?"

"Yes, doctor," Dr. Ingersoll answers.

Blue Apron returns pushing the cart that was beside the door. She wheels it up to the table, across from Dr. Strasburg. Paddy lifts his head.

"Down. Don't want to have to tell you again," Nurse McCormick hisses.

"Now, young fellow," Dr. Strasburg, stroking his black caterpillar, looks down at Paddy, "we are going to bandage your legs, first with dry gauze and then wet gauze. The wet gauze will then dry to form a plaster-of-Paris bandage—a cast. It won't hurt."

"A cast?"

"Casts—like trousers that get hard."

"Why?"

"To make you better, of course." Dr. Strasburg turns to Dr. Ingersoll. "Now, doctor lift his leg a little above the table. Flex the foot as I demonstrated."

"I don't want casts," Paddy sobs as he watches Blue Apron pass a bandage roll over him to Dr. Strasburg.

Closing his eyes, he feels the dry bandage being wrapped around his left foot and continuing slowly up and around his leg.

"Okay, your turn, Dr. Ingersoll," Dr. Strasburg says tying-off the bandage at the top of Paddy's thigh. "Make it neat and firm but not so tight as to cut off the circulation."

"Yes, yes, I know," Dr. Ingersoll answers.

Paddy opens his eyes and lifts his head as the doctors switch places.

"Lay back, Paddy," Nurse McCormick hisses again.

Paddy does as ordered.

When Dr. Ingersoll finishes wrapping the right foot and leg, Blue Apron takes two brown sacks from the cart and places one under each bandaged heel.

"The rod, Nurse Slaton," Dr. Strasburg orders.

Paddy sees a shiny bar being passed over him.

"Now hold the rod like this, Dr. Ingersoll, just above the ankles, while I fasten it with the gauze."

He feels the rod pushing against his legs as he watches Blue Apron lift a dripping wet bandage from the green bucket, wrings it out, and spreads it on top of the cart. Then, as if petting a kitten, she gently presses the bandage flat.

"Plaster bandage, please," Dr. Strasburg commands.

Again, Paddy lifts his head to look.

"Down, Paddy—down!" Nurse McCormick barks.

He plops back.

Blue Apron peels the bandage from the top of the cart and passes it to Dr. Strasburg. Paddy wiggles a little, feeling the cool mushiness wrapping around his left foot.

"Don't move, Paddy." Nurse McCormick squeezes his shoulder.

"I hate you," he moans, but to himself.

Wet bandage after wet bandage are passed to r. Strasburg. As he finishes encasing the left leg, Paddy hears him whisper under his breath while pressing lightly on wrapped knee, "Leg's bent-up some—should be okay."

He then turns to Dr. Ingersoll. "As you apply the plaster-of-Paris bandage, be sure the leg is kept completely straight."

While Dr. Ingersoll applies the plaster-of-Paris gauze to the right foot and leg, Paddy feels the wet bandage on the left foot and leg stiffening as the cast hardens. He wants to look, but Nurse McCormick's big scary eyes keep glaring down at him.

"Well, all finished, Paddy." Dr. Ingersoll smiles, waving his wet white hands over him.

"Can I look now?"

Dr. Strasburg nods. "Sure, young fellow."

Paddy scoots up on his elbows. "Gee—wow," he sighs.

The casts look to him like sticks of chalk held apart by a shiny bridge above his ankles. Far away his little pink toes stick up from the white plaster— as if now not a part of him.

"How long will I have them?" He looks up at Dr. Strasburg.

"A while," he answers.

Dr. Strasburg and Dr. Ingersoll then step away and walk toward the door while Blue Apron begins cleaning the table around Paddy's new white legs.

Paddy rests back, another rush of tears escaping his eyes.

"No sissy stuff. It's all over." Nurse McCormick smirks and wipes his cheeks with the back of her hand. "Now, stay still. The plaster must set. Don't move."

"Set! What's set? You said it was all over." Paddy pops up on his elbows.

"Set—get hard. And watch your tone with me. Lay down!"

He wants to bite her.

Waiting for the plaster to *set,* Paddy remains still while Nurse McCormick sits at a desk across the room. Her back is to him, but she turns occasionally to check on him. So, he doesn't move—not even a finger.

After a long while, he hears the silver doors open and the *clip-clopping* enter the room. He raises his head, just a little, as Johnny Cant pushes the gurney up beside him.

"How ya do'n'?" he asks.

"I got casts," Paddy says sadly.

Nurse McCormick calls over, not turning toward them. "They should be set by now. If so, he can go."

Johnny Cant presses the plaster-of-Paris with his finger, calling back, "Seems pretty set." He then bends over Paddy, saying softly, "Relax. I'm gonna slide ya from the table to the gurney."

"Okay," Paddy smiles, feeling so happy to be leaving the bad place.

* * *

Johnny Cant and Nurse Kelly together lift him from the gurney on to his bed. Nurse Kelly then slips brown sandbags under his ankles to raise the casts and props a pillow behind his head. As she does this, Paddy has his eyes on Johnny Cant who is digging into his pockets, like he has lost something.

Then, the giant smiles, two big gold teeth flash in the corners of his mouth. "Got something for ya." And he begins unraveling what looks like a bunch of string.

"What?" Paddy smiles back.

Holding up the string, his gold-teeth smile again, he says, "It's a magnet, but a swing'n magnet."

Dangling from the end of the string is a red and gold horseshoe, about the size of a silver dollar. Johnny Cant then tosses the magnet over the foot of the curtain railing surrounding the bed and carefully lowers it to where it's hanging from the string just beyond Paddy's far away toes.

"Now, here, ya take hold of the string an' pull it easy. Like this."

While Paddy holds the string, Johnny Cant gently moves his hand back and forth. And the red and gold horseshoe magnet begins swaying back and forth.

"See, if ya careful ya can get it swing'n nice an' steady like, and magnet will go higher and higher. Now, if yaw yank the it." He jerks on the string, causing the horseshoe to jump and stop moving. "It won't go. Ya gotta practice ta get it right."

With that, giant Johnny Cant takes his gurney and goes *clip-clopping* from the room, stooping so as not to hit his head on the top of the doorway.

"Bye," Paddy calls after him while he pulls the string and happily watches the swaying magnet.

"Well, isn't that a fine thing?" Nurse Kelly smiles and covers the white casts with a blanket. "Now, rest-up—you had a long mornin'."

Suddenly, the terrible cramps strike. They shoot through his legs—as if the polio is trying to break out of the casts. Paddy screams. The red and gold horseshoe magnet falls to the floor.

CHAPTER VI

Christmas Party
December 20, 1940
Day: Eighty-eight

Today is special. Paddy is going to a Christmas party—his first Christmas party, ever. He is wearing a sailor hat and sailor shirt. There are sailor pants as well, but as Nurse Kelly showed him, they can't slide up past the silver bar between the casts.

His mom and pop brought him the sailor suit when they visited for his fifth birthday, driving from Forrest Hills in their new car. "An auld jalopy," his mom grumbled, "wind up killin' us all".

Besides the sailor outfit, he got a box of *Crayolas*—"with every color under the sun, an' then some," his mom said. And Mr. Harmon sent along a package containing a *Red Ryder* coloring book and four *Red Ryder* comic books. The package was for Christmas, but his mom let him open it.

But the visit didn't start off well. When they first arrived and saw the casts, his mom cried while his pop got angry—"blewdy mess," he said. But they soon cheered-up; particularly when Paddy told them that he was no longer having cramps. And they had a good laugh when he recited the funny rhyme Mr. Martin taught him as a birthday present:

Thirty days has September,
April, June and no wonder,
All the rest eat peanut butter,
'Cept grandma,
She rides a tricycle.

* * *

Peering out the window while waiting for Johnny Cant, Paddy searches as he does every day to see if the squirrels are back. They're not, just loads of snow. Nurse Edelstein says they're all cuddled together keeping warm in a nest high up in the big tree.

He hears the gurney coming—*clip-clop, clip-clop*. The wheel's still broke.

"Ya ready?" Johnny Cant says, ducking through the doorway pushing the gurney, Nurse Kelly behind him.

"Yeah. Like my sailor suit?" Paddy calls to him.

"Swell, Champ. Real swell."

Champ. That's what Johnny Cant calls him since he can now make the horseshoe magnet swing up almost to the ceiling—higher than anyone can, Johnny Cant says. So, he's a Champ. Paddy likes that.

"Now," Nurse Kelly covers his legs with a blanket while Johnny Cant slides him on to the gurney, "you have yerself a lovely time—and no scratching there above your casts. The ointment will calm the etch—but not cure it. You must leave it be or it will get worst."

"Okay—sure," he answers, anxious to get going.

As Johnny Cant then pushes the gurney from the room, Paddy turns, looking up at him.

"Where's it at, the Christmas party?"

"The auditorium."

"Auditorium?"

"Yup. A big room off Broadway. Got a stage, a balcony, too. Ya'll see."

Broadway is the longest of the many hallways, all of which have names. The one outside Paddy's room is Thruway. The solarium is off Main Street. He goes there several times a week, puts on dark glasses, and lies almost naked under a large hot lamp. "Boring, boring, boring," he complains to Nurse Kelly after each solarium session. And where some of the hallways meet is called Times Square.

As soon as they turn on to Broadway, the longest hallway, Paddy hears it—the laughing and talking, getting louder and louder as the gurney *clip-clops* along. They finally push through the two large doors into the auditorium—the clamor is almost deafening!

"Holy Cow!" Paddy shouts to Jonny Cant.

"Yup! It's som'n, Champ," he shouts back.

Kids are everywhere—in chairs, in the aisles, up in the balcony, along the walls in wheelchairs and on gurneys. On the stage is a Christmas tree—rising to the high ceiling—sparkling with lights of all different colors and topped with a blinking blue star.

Johnny Cant wheels the gurney to the rear of the auditorium, under the balcony. There, he backs it up against the wall near a gurney with young girl sitting on it. She has long blond hair, pulled into a ponytail and tied with a red ribbon matching her red sweater. Her legs, like Paddy's, are covered with a brown blanket.

She turns to him, her eyes large, blue, and unblinking like a doll. She smiles. Paddy grins shyly and turns quickly away, thinking: *Wow. She's pretty—really pretty.*

The auditorium slowly darkens, except for the Christmas tree which seems even brighter. Then, from behind the tree, kids in Santa hats begin appearing and walking across the stage, most using crutches or canes.

"What's that on their legs?" Paddy looks to Johnny Cant who is behind him leaning against the wall.

"Whose legs?"

"Them, up there." He points.

"Braces."

"Braces?"

"Yeah, helps 'em to walk."

"Oh." Paddy turns back to the front of the auditorium.

As the Santa kids line up across the stage, everyone gradually sits down. It gets quiet—except for three boys in the last row of seats, directly in front of Paddy. They're standing—laughing and shoving one another. As he watches, a nurse rushes up behind them. He knows right away they're in trouble. It's Nurse McCormick!

Without a word, she slaps the back of the red head of the center, knocking his chin to his chest. He whirls around with a yelp, looking as if to hit her back.

"You naughty boys! Sit! Be quiet!" Nurse McCormick barks.

The redhead looks away, sliding slowly down in his seat as the two companions do the same. Turning from them, Nurse McCormick glances toward Paddy. His heart jumps. He turns away from her. She walks off.

Then when her back is to the naughty boys, the redhead jumps to his feet. Thumbs in his ears, he wiggles his fingers at her and sticks out his tongue. Paddy's heart jumps again: *She'll turn for sure—she'll catch him.*

He looks anxiously at the pretty girl, who is giggling at him from behind her hands as if they're in cahoots with the naughty boys. Paddy smiles nervously and looks back at the redhead who is slumped down in his seat, quietly looking toward the stage.

On the stage, Santa kids in wheelchairs are now rolling out from behind the Christmas tree and lining up in front of the walk-on Santa kids. After them, a lady in a long blue dress comes out. She goes across the stage and sits down at a piano. It's quiet now, church quiet.

Suddenly, from behind the Christmas tree comes a booming, "HO! HO! HO!"

Everyone starts clapping—the naughty boys are on their feet hooting and shaking their fists in the air. Santa Claus, with a big red sack over his shoulder, rushes across the stage: "HO! HO! HO!"

Halfway, he stops, drops the sack, bows to the audience, and spinning around, he raises his arms to the Santa kids. It's then quiet again. Not the naughty boys, though. They stay standing, laughing, and shoving. But Nurse McCormick is on them in a second, twisting the redhead's ear. He squeals. The naughty boys all drop into their seats.

"Shut up! Sit down! This is the last time I'll tell you," she hisses and walks off, not looking at Paddy this time.

The redhead goes to waggle his fingers at her, but the buddy on his right him pulls down his hands as the piano strikes a note. Paddy looks to the stage as Santa Claus swings his arms down. The Santa kids burst out singing:

Jingle Bells,
Jingle Bells,
Jingle all the way,
Oh! What fun it is to ride,
In a one horse, open sleigh.

Christmas song after Christmas song is sung. Some just the Santa kids sing. Some everyone sings. Mostly, Paddy make-believe sings, not knowing the words, while smiling every so often at the pretty girl. She always smiles back: *She's swell—really swell!*

When all the singing ends, Santa Claus turns around. He bows. The audience claps like mad. He points to the piano player. She stands and bows. They clapping gets louder and all the kids sitting in chairs rise—the naughty boys spring to their feet and start stomping their feet. Santa Claus turns back to the Santa kids. He raises his arms. The Santa kids wave. Everyone claps and claps while other kids begin stomping along with the naughty boys.

Santa Claus then throws his sack over his shoulder and marches across the stage waving and bellowing, "HO! HO! HO!"

As he disappears behind the Christmas tree, the clapping gradually stops—but not the stomping. It goes on, the thunderous pounding shaking the balcony over Paddy's head. Then a long, shrill sound, like the whistle of a kettle at full boil, penetrates the clamor. And Nurse McCormick appears from under the balcony. And with short, violent steps, she rushes down the center aisle of the auditorium, her cheeks puffing out with each blast of her whistle.

She stops before the stage, spins around to face *her* audience—whistle blasting. The stompers stop, immediately. Those standing sit down. The whistle goes silent and drops from Nurse McCormick's mouth to a string around her neck. Quiet—you could hear a pin drop. She starts walking slowly back up the aisle, her threatening eyes darting up and down, side to side. Behind her, the walking Santa kids begin leaving the stage to fill empty seats in the front rows while those in wheelchairs move to the back of the stage.

Paddy glances at the naughty boys. They have their heads bowed, as if in prayer. He hears them, though, snickering. He looks at the pretty girl. She grins at him—her face scarlet, as if about to burst. She turns away, burying her face in her hands.

A voice comes from the stage: "Good evening, boys and girls! And Merry Christmas to you all!"

Paddy turns to see a man in a black suit and a Santa hat standing where Santa Claus was. He waits a moment while the last of the Santa kids are in their seats. Then, he starts talking.

His name, he says, is Dr. Ryan, and he's the Director of the Reconstruction Home, and he rambles on and on telling how great the hospital is, how it has great clinics and a great swimming pool, how the nurses, the doctors, and all the staff are the greatest.

All the while, Paddy has his eyes on the naughty boys who are now busy making faces at each other. The redhead also keeps turning to smile at the pretty girl. Each time she smiles back—Paddy wishing she wouldn't.

When Dr. Ryan finally finishes, a women in a red dress walks from the audience up on to the stage. Everyone applauds, but not near as wildly as for Santa Claus. She begins talking, saying she's happy to be at their Christmas party and that God loves them, and that she loves them, too. She then tells them "her very best of all" Christmas story.

When she finishes, there's more applause. And the naughty boys stay in their seats clapping nicely—with Nurse McCormick standing right behind them. The lady in the red dress bows and wishes everyone a Merry Christmas. With that, the auditorium lights brighten and all at once everyone starts leaving.

"We'll stay put till it clears out some," Johnny Cant calls to Paddy from his place against the wall.

As they wait, Paddy watches the three naughty boys move out from their aisle, laughing and jabbing each other with their crutches. The redhead keeps looking back at the pretty girl. She smiles, big smiles, at him. Paddy keeps hoping she'll smile at him like that, too. She doesn't.

At the end of the aisle, Nurse McCormick, her arms wrapped across her chest, is waiting for the naughty boys. She says something to them as they file out. They stop laughing. Then, when past her, they race away, laughing again, their braced legs swinging forward pendulum-like between their crutches. Nurse McCormick hurries after them. Something then bumps Paddy's gurney, drawing his eyes from the Nurse McCormick and the naughty boys.

"Sorry," the pretty girl says as a nurse pushes her gurney by his.

"It's okay—it's okay," Paddy mumbles shyly.

With a little smile she looks back at him and waves, sending tingles all through him.

"Let's go now," Paddy calls apprehensively to Johnny Cant. "Let's follow that gurney—with the blond girl."

"Hold ya horses just a bit more."

"No. Please, I want to follow that gurney!" he persists.

"Relax, champ—no big rush."

Three more gurneys go by, and they at last move out. At the auditorium doors, Santa Claus is greeting each boy and girl as they leave. Just beyond him, Paddy can see the pretty girl starting down Broadway.

"Merry Christmas, Paddy," Santa says handing him a small blue box decorated with white stars when his turn comes. *Sounds kind-a like Dr. Ingersoll,* Paddy thinks, looking up at the white bearded face.

46

"What 'bout candy for me, Santa?" Johnny Cant smiles with a flash of gold teeth.

"Ho-ho-ho," Santa Claus says, tossing him a box.

The pretty girl is now far ahead, almost at the end of Broadway, as they move on.

"Go fast—please," Paddy urges Johnny Cant.

"What's the rush?" He drops his box of candy on Paddy's lap. "Here, an extra for ya—keep ya mind off the girls."

She turns from Broadway and is gone.

* * *

"...then this lady told us a story about St. Nicholas—who's really Santa Claus—and how he flies down from the sky in a sleigh pulled by tiny reindeer with funny names, jumps down a chimney, gets all dirty, and laughs, shaking all over—like jelly—and fills stockings with toys and candy. He then touches his nose and shoots back up the chimney flying away shouting Happy Christmas."

"Sound like you had great fun—but you must calm down a little," Nurse Kelly says, slipping off Paddy's sailor shirt.

After being quiet for a few moments, he asks, less excitedly, "Where did all the kids come from?"

"From here, where else?"

She folds his shirt neatly and places it on his nightstand beside the sailor hat and unused sailor pants.

"But where, where are they? I never see them."

"They're in wards."

"What wards?"

"Big long rooms with beds lined up one after another on each side."

"There's lot of them—kids?"

"Oh, indeed. Now, will you not offer me another sweet?"

"They have polio, also?" he hands her the box of candies.

"No. Most have other problems, God bless 'em."

"Why don't I see them—except sometimes in the hallways?"

"Well, as you saw at the party, they're older than you—a lot older." She sits on the side of his bed fishing around in the candy box. "Sure, yer the baby in the house."

"I'm not a baby! I'm five!"

"That you are—growin' up fast, too. But yer'ill always be me baby."

She gently pinches his cheek and pops a candy into her mouth.

He pushes her hand away. "Can I play with them?"

"Ooo, now, they're awful busy with school, therapy, an' all that."

"Wow—there's a school here?"

"Oh, sure. They're taught the basics an' some skills—makin' baskets, sewin', wood shop, an' the like."

"Can I go to school?"

"No. Yer too young, yet."

"I want to go stay in a ward then not in this stupid room all by myself."

"Now, that's not up to me. But do you really want that?"

"Yes!"

"They can be a rowdy bunch, some of the boys, as you told me yerself. Yer're better off where yer at."

"The pretty girl's not rowdy. I'll stay in her ward. She likes me—a lot. She could be my best friend."

"Enough, now," Nurse Kelly laughs, standing up from the bed. "No more of your blathering. Rest a bit. Mr. Martin will be by soon with your supper."

CHAPTER VII

Ma Gillick
January 2, 1941
Day: One Hundred and One

"Hello there."

Paddy looks up from his coloring as a woman with short, dark curly hair and wearing a white doctor's jacket walks into the room.

She slides a chair up beside his bed. "What's that you're coloring?"

"A horse." He shows her the picture.

"It's a lovely horse."

She leans over him, smelling nice like *Chiclets Gum*, and looks at the picture.

"It's Thunder. Red Ryder's horse," Paddy explains.

"And this is quite an assortment of crayons you have," she says, picking up the Crayola box.

"Got them for my birthday from Mom and Pop."

"So you had a nice Christmas visit with your parents?"

"No. They didn't come. They came for my birthday—before Christmas."

"Oh. But you went to the Christmas party?" she asks, placing the Crayola box on the nightstand.

"Yes, it was great. I got candy, too. Two boxes. Johnny Cant gave me his. We ate one box already, Nurse Kelly and me. Did you go?"

"I did. You saw me. I played the piano."

"That was you. Holy cow! You looked different—but you played good."

"Well, thank you. Let's put your coloring aside for now, and let me tell you why I'm here."

"Sure." He closes the coloring book on his lap.

"My name is Ma Gillick. Ma—for Martha."

She takes the coloring book and puts it under the Crayola box on his nightstand.

"Mine's Paddy." He extends his hand—like his pop would.

She shakes it gently, smiling.

"I'm what we call a physiotherapist."

"You're not a nurse—didn't think so. You have no hat."

"No, I'm not a nurse. My job is to help you walk again."

"Walk again—you mean really walk?" He scoots himself up in the bed feeling a rush of excitement.

"Yes, we're going to wake up the muscles in those legs of yours. Time to put them back to work."

"But I have casts?"

"Don't you worry about that. May I look at your legs?"

"Sure," he answers happily.

Ma Gillick stands, slides down his covers, and slowly pulls his gown up. He holds his breath, but it's okay. She doesn't pull it up too far.

"Wiggle your right toes?"

Sticking out of the cast, his right toes wiggle.

"And the left ones."

"I can't," he says, only half trying to move them.

"Wiggle your left toes," Ma Gillick repeats sternly.

"I can't. They don't work." He grunts, trying harder.

"*Can't*—not a good word."

She takes his left toes and gently moves them back and forth. She then slides his gown up just a little more and touches the red skin at the top of the left cast.

"Ouch." He flinches.

"You shouldn't be scratching yourself."

"Nurse Kelly, she tells me not to, too, and puts stuff there so it won't itch so much—but it still does."

"No more scratching." She gives him a serious look. "I want the redness gone the next time I see you. Understand?"

"I'll try."

"*Try*—that's not a good word either. Just don't scratch."

Paddy nods.

"Do your legs still cramp?"

"Sometimes."

"When was the last time?"

"I don't remember."

"Well, that'll do for now." She quickly pulls down his gown and covers him.

"That's all?" He grumbles disappointedly.

Placing her soft hand on the back of Paddy's neck, she leans over and kisses his forehead. "Yes, Paddy, that's all for now. I'll be seeing you again very soon."

Watching Ma Gillick turn away and walk to the door, he calls out, "You really going to help me walk?"

"I am." She looks back at him.

"When?"

"Soon."

"Bye!" He calls after her wishing she would stay longer.

"Bye, Paddy!"

She waves. Paddy waves back, thinking happily: She's nice. Pretty, too. Almost prettier than the Christmas party girl. And she's really going to help me walk—walk again.

Ma Gillick disappears into the hallway.

CHAPTER VIII

Bye, Bye, Mr. Plaster-of-Paris
January 10, 1941
Day: One Hundred and Nine

"You look like your sufferin' from a double dose of original sin," Nurse Kelly grumbles as she props two pillows against Paddy's back, allowing him to twist a little to his side and take the pressure off the recovering bed sores on his bottom.

"Better?" she asks.

"Still hurts," he mumbles.

"Now, won't you tell me what's botherin' you?"

"Nothing. I told you that already."

"Sure there is. An' if you would tell me, maybe it'll make you feel better."

"No! What's that, *original sin*?"

"Never mind—the priests will be layin' that on you soon enough. Now cheer up—be back later."

Paddy turns his attention to the window when she leaves to see if the squirrels are back. They're not, just heaps of snow on the ground and the y always-gray sky. Thinking dejectedly—*they're never coming back, like Ma. Gillick didn't*—he hears the *clip-clop, clip-clop, clip-clop* in the hallway.

He looks to the door as the gurney rolls into the room.

"Hay, Champ," Johnny Cant says cheerily, ducking through the doorway.

"Go away," Paddy pouts.

Johnny Cant moves the gurney up beside the bed, lifts Paddy on to it, and tosses one of the ugly brown blankets over his legs.

Lying back, Paddy closes his eyes, thinking, We're going to the stupid, boring, boring, boring solarium.

At Times square, he senses the gurney turning in the opposite direction from the solarium. He opens his eyes and slides up on his elbows. A moment later, the gurney pushes through the silver doors into the casting room. And there standing by the steel table watching him approach are Dr. Ingersoll and Blue Apron with her cast cart.

"What are you going to do?" Paddy asks, his heart now racing as the gurney slides up beside the table.

"Your casts are coming off," Dr. Ingersoll says, not in his Santa Claus voice.

"I'm getting new ones?"

"No. They're going—gone for good."

"Now?" Paddy looks from the doctor to Blue Apron, who nods her head in agreement.

"Right now," Dr. Ingersoll says. "The casts have been hiding those legs of yours for what, four months? Time we get rid of 'em, don't you think?"

"Yeah!" Paddy explodes as Johnny Cant lifts him gently him on to the cold table.

"You remember Nurse Slaton," Dr. Ingersoll says, removing the brown blanket and sliding Paddy's gown up.

"Hi." He smiles at Blue Apron, who covers his hips with a towel.

"So," Dr. Ingersoll ruffles Paddy's hair, "let's do it."

"Can I watch?"

"Sure, no extra charge."

"Me, too, doctor?" asks Johnny Cant, standing a little away from the table.

"For you, it'll be a-dollar-two-eighty." Dr. Ingersoll chuckles.

Johnny Cant moves to the head of the table while Blue Apron goes to the other end and places brown sandbags under Paddy's heels, raising his casted legs from the surface.

"We'll start on the left leg, Nurse Slaton," Dr. Ingersoll says, lifting giant scissors from the top of the cart. "Hold the leg steady."

He then looks down at Paddy. "Ready?"

"Yes, okay," Paddy murmurs, holding tight to the sides of the table while gazing uneasily at the big scissors.

"This won't hurt. Just may pinch a little."

Dr. Ingersoll then slides the tip of the scissor blade between the cast and Paddy's little toe, sending a cold shiver shooting up his leg. He tenses, jerking himself back a little.

"Just relax." Dr. Ingersoll glances at him.

Paddy watches anxiously as the scissor begins to cut slowly from his little toe along the outside of his foot. It then turns slightly pressing against his ankle—he flinches, squeezing the table. The blade moves on up his leg, sprinkling a snowy trail of plaster dust on the table.

"Ouch!" The sharp tip pokes his knee.

"Want-a-rest?" Dr. Ingersoll stops cutting.

"No—no. Keep going," Paddy responds quickly.

At the top of his thigh, where Paddy's scratched skin is still red, Dr. Ingersoll makes a final snip of the cast and hands the scissors to Blue Apron.

"Spreader, please," he then says, inspecting the long slit in the plaster.

Blue Apron passes him another big scissor from the cart. This one has flat tips. Holding it up, Dr. Ingersoll smiles at him, "Now, let's pop it open."

Paddy grips the table.

With Blue Apron steadying the cast, Dr. Ingersoll jiggles the flat spreader tips into the split cast just above Paddy's knee. He slowly pulls the spreader blades apart. The cast squeaks like a rusty hinge, and then with a sharp branch cracking sound, it splits open.

"Wow!" Paddy gasps, seeing his bare leg lying between the chunks of white plaster like a pink hotdog in a bun.

"One down, one to go." Dr. Ingersoll eyes Paddy while he moves to the other side of the table. "Doing okay, fella?"

"Yes." Paddy grins wearily.

The right cast is cut the same way—but no "ouch" this time—and split open. Going then to the end of the table, Dr. Ingersoll removes the brown sandbags from under the busted open plaster.

"Now, Paddy," he says, "I'm going to slide the casts out from under you. Okay?"

"Uh-huh." he nods.

Gripping the silver bar with one hand, Dr. Ingersoll slowly pulls away the split casts, letting the bare legs slide gently on to the table. Paddy sighs, feeling the wonderfully cool, metal surface against his skin.

Then, lifting the silver bar up in the air—a split-open leg cast dangling from each end—Dr. Ingersoll laughs, swaying the ruminants from side to side. "It's goodbye to Mr. Plaster-of-Paris."

"Bye, bye." Paddy laughs.

Placing the rubble on top of the cart, Dr. Ingersoll moves again to the side of the table as he and Paddy gaze curiously at the withered limbs. To Paddy, they look fake: *toy legs,* the words pop into his mind.

Dr. Ingersoll places his hand on the left knee, which is bent up off the table. He presses down. Paddy screams— it's as if the knee had been struck with a hammer—and collapses back on to the table.

"Damn!" Dr. Ingersoll jerks his hand away. "I'm sorry, Paddy!"

"It's okay! It's okay!" he sobs as the pain quickly subsides.

"I won't do that again." The doctor gently pats the top of the knee. "Now, want to try moving your toes for me?"

"Sure." Paddy sits up a little dizzily and wipes away a few tears trickling down his cheeks.

His right toes wiggle, as they did for Ma Gillick. The left ones still don't move. Dr. Ingersoll shakes his head, seeming angry.

"Did I do good?" Paddy asks anxiously.

The doctor's hand brushes Paddy's hair. "You did fine—excellent! Now, I'll leave you in Nurse Slaton's hands."

He then turns and walks away toward the sink. Blue Apron follows him taking the casts from the cart which she dumps in a garbage can by the door.

"Take care, Paddy. You did good—real good." Dr. Ingersoll strolls from the sink to the door after washing his hands. "I'll be seeing you again soon."

"Bye, Dr. Ingersoll." Paddy waves.

Blue Apron returns to the table with a towel over her arm and carrying a basin of water.

"I'll clean you up some, Paddy," she says, her first words to him, and she smiles, too.

Taking a small brush and dustpan from her cart, she lifts Paddy's legs—her touch feeling so wonderfully soft—and sweeps the bits of plaster and snowy powder from under them. Then, she cleans each leg—the warm, damp cloth sending lovely goose bumps all through him.

* * *

"I know. I know. I saw it, too," Johnny Cant says, as Paddy rattles on explaining how Dr. Ingersoll cut the casts away. "I was right there—remember? Sounds ta me like ya gonna miss 'em."

"No, I won't!" Paddy turns up at him from the gurney with an affected mean look.

"Well, just in case ya do start missin' em, here's some'n ta maybe keep ya mind off ya loss—and ta shut ya up for a while."

Johnny Cant pulls a rolled-up comic book from his pocket and tosses it on to Paddy's lap. On the cover is a man with a big *S* on his chest and a red cape flying behind him. He has his hands on his hips, legs apart, like watching something happening far away—something bad.

"Wow, who's that?"

"Who's that? That's Superman. Says so right there at the top of the page."

"Superman? He got a horse?" Paddy asks, flipping through the pages.

"A horse! Superman—a horse?" Johnny Cant laughs, swinging the gurney into Paddy's room. "He don't need no horse; he can fly."

After quickly settling Paddy in his bed, the giant turns his gurney towards the door. "See ya, Champ."

"Bye," Paddy answers, his eyes glued to the picture of Superman. "Thanks a lot."

"Ya welcome."

As soon as Johnny Cant leaves, Paddy pages slowly through his first *Superman* comic book, delighting in feeling its light weight sitting across his legs. He then put the comic book aside, lifts the covers, peeps under and smiles, whispering Dr. Ingersoll's delightful words: *Bye, bye Mr. Plaster-of Paris.*

CHAPTER IX

The H.M. Cutter Yacht Britannia
January 18, 1941
Day: One Hundred and Seventeen

Hearing footsteps coming into the room, Paddy looks up from his Superman comic—the unexpected sight and familiar voice taking his breath away.

"Paddy, me darlin'—an' aren't you lookin' gran'."

"Mom! Pop!" He shouts. "Holy Cow!"

"How you do'n, son?" his pop calls out.

"Oh, so wonderful to see you." His mom all smiles coming up to his bed. She leans over and kisses his cheek.

"And you know who this is?" His pop says loudly, turning back to the doorway.

Paddy looks past him to see a man in a wearing a peaked sailor cap coming into the room carrying a large sack.

"It's your Uncle Jack—all the way from Liverpool, England, to see you."

Uncle Jack walks to Paddy's bed, places his sack on the end of it, and comes up beside him extending his hand. Paddy gazes in wonder at his big rugged face with thick, black eyebrows, his gold buttoned jacket, and the great hat.

"Pleased to meet you, lad." He smiles, thin lines forming at the corners of his gray eyes.

"Hi." Paddy smiles back, shaking Uncle's Jack's rough hand.

"Your Uncle Jack's in the British Merchant Service—ship's carpenter," his pop says happily.

Uncle Jack removes his cap, drops it beside Paddy. As coats are removed and placed on the empty bed, he picks the cap up and carefully inspects it. It has a white top. On the front of the white top is a heavy, black cloth badge embodied with a gold crown at the top, green garlands circling down from the crown around the edge, and a small red anchor sown in the center. Separating the white top and a shiny black peak is a gold rope. *Real keen*, Paddy smiles, running his finger across the velvety badge.

"Now, how are yer legs?" his mom asks, pulling a chair up beside the bed.

"The casts are gone. They took them off."

"Oh, lovely. When was that?" she says, sitting down.

"Last week."

"Let me see."

"No. No. Not now—Uncle Jack." Paddy looks toward his uncle and his pop who are looking out the window at the falling snow.

"Casts are off—what I 'ear?" His pop turns from the window and comes up beside Paddy's bed. "Let's have a look."

He reaches to pull down his covers. Paddy drops the cap and grabs his pop's hand, "No, Pop!"

"Bill, later perhaps," Nan says, looking up at her husband.

"Ah, a quick look."

"No, please, Pop," Paddy pleads, glancing over at Uncle Jack still looking out the window.

"Bill." His mom pokes him in the leg with her elbow. "For the love of God, have you no sense at all!"

"'E don't mind, do you, son?"

"Bill, no!" Nan elbows Bill again as he tugs his hand free of his son's grip.

"It's okay, Mom. Don't fight," Paddy mummers.

"Dense as a tinker's donkey." Nan grumbles angrily.

Bill slides the cover down and pulls his son's gown up. Paddy presses the sailor cap into his lap to stop him from going too far. Nan moves forward in her chair as Uncle Jack steps over from the window.

For a long moment, they all gaze in silence at the naked legs.

Finally, with a deep sigh, Nan says, "So thin, Bill. No more than twigs."

"Aye." He nods.

"Look sound 'enough to me," says Uncle Jack, glancing at Paddy from under his shaggy eyebrows.

Bill places his hand on Paddy's left thigh. Paddy cringes at the cool touch.

"Don't know, Jack. Not much muscle 'ear, far as I can tell."

He slides his hand down to the knee.

"No, Pop." Paddy reaches for his father's hand

"Bowed up a bit as well." Bill presses down.

Paddy screeches, the piercing pain shooting through his knee.

His pop jerks his hand away as if feeling the painful shock himself.

"Didn't mean to hurt you, son!"

"Oh, God help us!" Nan shouts. "What have you done, Bill!"

"I did noth'n!" He turns angrily to her.

"It's-okay-Mom-it's-okay," Paddy stutters as the dizzying pain quickly subsides.

"Bill! Cover the child! We've seen enough—we have!"

"O' aye." He sighs, sliding the nightgown down and carefully replacing Paddy's covers. "Sorry, son." He pats Paddy's head.

"It's okay, Pop." Paddy smiles gamely, holding back his tears.

"Now, let's see what we 'ave here for the lad," Uncle Jack's voice rings out cheerfully from the end of Paddy's bed. He starts to open his big sack then stops, looking at Paddy as if there was something wrong.

"'Alf-a-mo!" he says.

He moves from the end of the bed, lifts his cap from Paddy's lap, and places it on the boy's head. Paddy smiles, feeling the cap drooping over his ears while smelling its hair tonic odor. Uncle Jack then takes out a small gold pin from his vest pocket. He holds it up to Paddy between his thumb and finger.

"Lad, this here is the lapel pin worn proudly by every seaman in the British Merchant Service." He moves the pin closer. "The crown engraved there at the top—that's for our King, George VI."

"Like the one on the cap badge?" Paddy says, looking carefully at the pin.

"Aye, that's right, smart lad," Uncle Jack smiles. "The circle of braided rope, below the crown, see?"

"Yes."

"That rope stands for the sea and ships. And the MN—'ere in the center of the rope." He points at the letters. "That's for Merchant Navy."

He leans over, attaches the pin to Paddy's nightgown, and pats it gently. Stepping back, Uncle Jack looks from hat to pin. "Now," he smiles, "the lad's properly attired to take delivery of what's in me sack. Don't you think, Bill?"

"O' aye." Bill chuckles.

Returning to the end of the bed, Uncle Jack slides his hands down deep into his sack, saying with a deep voice, "Up from the depths o' the sea—the *H.M. Cutter Yacht Britannia!*"

"Holy cow!" Paddy cries out as white sails rise from the bag. "A boat!"

Lifting the *H.M. Cutter Yacht Britannia* from his sack, Uncle Jack steps forward and places it between Paddy's legs, the sails rising higher than the boy's head.

"She's all plank and frame, son," his pop says, reaching over to help hold up the *Britannia*.

"Aye." Uncle Jack taps the yacht's shiny wood side, making a drumming sound. "You see, Paddy, she's hollow inside. Each wood plank form'n the hull, as well as the deck, is glued and tacked to a frame. 'Ere, take a look through the hatch."

He removes the three hatch covers. Each is a shiny brown, but a darker than the almost white wood deck.

"Gee," Paddy mutters, looking down in through the hatch cover into the hull, the smell the glue and fresh wood rising up.

"The sails," Uncle Jack says, replacing the hatch covers, "are made from genuine sail cloth."

He names them; pointing to each, "Top sail. Main sail. Jibs."

"And the fixtures," his pop adds, "they're all solid brass."

"Boy, it's a great boat, really great," Paddy says, feeling the heavy cloth sails. "Does it float?"

"Blewdy 'ell better!" Uncle Jack laughs. "She's caulked well and sealed with five coats of lacquer. And the keel 'ere," he taps it, "is mostly lead. She'll stay upright in a good blow."

"It's lovely, Jack." Nan reaches over in her chair and slides her fingers along the smooth hull.

"Aye, thank you, Nan," Uncle Jack answers while removing a pipe and tobacco pouch from his pants pocket. "She's a three-sixteenth inch scale copy. True to the original in every detail—which was a hundred feet in length with a hundred and ten foot main mast."

He flips open his pouch, quickly fills his pipe, lights it, and continues. "And she has an interesting history."

"Oh, and how's that, Jack?" Nan says looking up and him.

"Well, she was built for the Prince of Wales and launched in 1892, soon to become one of the most celebrated rac'n yachts of all time. But she came to a bad end."

"A bad end?" Nan says resting back in her chair watching Paddy happily moving the mainsail back and forth.

"Yes indeed. The Prince of Wales—he later became King Edward VII—when he died, the *Britannia* was inherited by his son, George V who tended to 'er pretty well. But when 'e died, that was in 1936, none of 'is sons wanted to keep her up. So rejected and go'n to ruin, the *Britannia* was one day stripped of her mast and gear and towed into the deep waters off the Isle o' Wright. And there she was scuttled."

"Scuttled—they sunk it?"

"Aye, Nan, they did," Uncle Jack puffs his pipe, "right to the bottom of the English Channel."

"Wouldn't you know?" Nan shakes her head. "Al' daft—Kings, Queens, Dukes, an' Dunces—the lot of 'em."

"Nan," Uncle Jack blows a circle of smoke, "you may 'ave some'n there. And now, Paddy," he turns to him, "I must correct you. You made an error in refer'n to the *Britannia*."

"I did? I'm sorry," Paddy replies, trying to think what the error might be.

"Aye—a minor point but important for men of the sea. You don't call the *Britannia* a boat. A rowboat, that's a boat. A submarine, that's called a boat as well. The *Britannia,* she's a yacht—or a ship if you like—never a boat."

"A yacht—ship." Paddy nods, stroking the white main sail.

"And the yacht is not a *he,* always a *she,*" his pop adds.

"What rubbish," Nan grumbles softly.

"Correct, Bill," Uncle Jack says. "And, Paddy, I also built a stand for *her.*"

Returning to the end of the bed, pipe clinched in his teeth, he digs once more into his sack removing the stand, shiny light colored wood like the deck.

"Let's see how she'll look," Bill says.

Uncle Jack passes the stand to him, and he places it on Paddy's nightstand. Then, taking the yacht from between his son's legs, he sets her carefully in place.

"Ah, that'll do just fine—you think, Paddy?" Bill smiles, stepping back to admire the beautiful *H.M. Cutter Yacht Britannia!*

"Yes. Can I keep it there, Pop?"

"Sure, why not?" his mom answers. "It'll add bit of life to the dreary place."

"Aye," his pop agrees. Then, turning to Uncle Jack, he says, "What you say, Jack, give you a tour of the place?"

"Splendid idea."

"Back in two-shake-of-the-lambs-tail, Paddy," his pop says happily as he and Uncle Jack gather up their coats and stroll from the room.

As soon as the men leave, Paddy tells his mom all about the great Christmas party: the pretty girl, the singing, the naughty boys, the foot stomping, mean Nurse McCormick, the Santa candies at the end—and how all the kids are in wards, and that Nurse Kelly said he's a baby and can't be with them.

He then describes how Dr. Ingersoll took the casts off and wiggled them in the air. He shows her the *Superman* comic Johnny Cant gave him when it was all over, complaining that Nurse Edelstein calls the comic "trash" but still reads it to him sometimes when he does well in his lessons.

His mom wants to know all about that, but also the lessons. So Paddy explains how, after supper, Nurse Edelstein is teaching him the alphabet and counting and reads stories to him from books—like last night, she read *The Emperor's New Clothes,* explaining to his mom that it was mostly a funny story but sad, too, because everyone laughs at Emperor.

After that, Paddy himself gets sad while telling her about Ma Gillick coming and saying she will help him walk again—and then never coming back. He cries a little—but stops right away when they heard the men returning down the hallway laughing. And his mom quickly wiped away his tears.

"Get'n wicked out," Bill announces as he and Uncle Jack enter the room. "Best be on our way soon, Nan."

"In a bit, Bill," Nan replies.

Pulling her chair close to the bed, she grumbles, "They've been drinkin'—can smell, I can. A bottle in the ol' jalopy, no doubt."

She then takes Paddy's hand saying softly, "Now, darlin', there's something you must do every night before you go to sleep an' every mornin' right when you wake up."

"Okay," he answers, also softly, as if they're having a secret.

"You must make the *Sign-of-the-Cross* on each of your legs, like this."

She traces her finger over Paddy's left thigh, then the right one.

"An' you say this special prayer: *Blessed Virgin Mary Mother of God make my legs well.* Can you promise ter do that?"

"Yes, Mom." He glances at Pop and Uncle Jack who are staring out the window at the blowing snow.

"Do it now—show me."

Paddy slides his hand from her hand and makes the *Sign-of-the-Cross* on his left and then his right thigh.

"An' you say?"

"Blessed Virgin Mary Mother of God makes my legs well."

"You promise now, to do it every night before you go to sleep an' every mornin' right when you wake up."

"Yes." Paddy nods.

"Say it—say I promise."

"I promise."

"Good, Paddy."

She sits back, smiling brightly, and takes her pocketbook from where it's hanging on the back of the chair. Opening it, she removes a small, green cloth pouch. From the pouch, she pulls out a thin silver chain with a silver medal at the end of it.

With the medal in her palm, the chain hanging down from her hand, she again leans close in toward Paddy.

"Here is a holy medal, blessed by Monsignor Higgins 'imself—God love 'im. On this side, you see, is the image of the *Most Blessed Virgin Mary*. That's to remind you of yer special prayer an' yer special promise. An' here," she turns the holy medal over, "is the image of the *Sacred Heart of Jaysus*—representing love an' courage."

Unclasping the silver chain, she places the holy medal around her son's small neck.

"You must wear this all the time an' kiss it after you say the special prayer."

She then lifts the holy medal from Paddy's chest, kisses the image of the *Most Blessed Virgin Mary,* kisses his cheek, and sets the holy medal back in place.

Paddy looks down at the holy medal and at the special British Merchant Service lapel pin pinned to his gown thinking happily: *They're snazzy, real snazzy.*

* * *

"And go right to sleep now. You had a long day." Nurse Edelstein turns out the lights.

"You really like the *Britannia*?" Paddy asks, looking over at the tall sails all bright in the moonlight streaming in the window.

"Yes, it's a fine boat," she says and disappears into the hallway.

"It's not a boat." He calls after her. "And it's, *she's,* a yacht or a ship."

Unclasping the British Merchant Service lapel pin, he reaches over and places it on the *Britannia*'s deck. Then, sliding down deep under the covers, he makes the *Sign-of-the-Cross* on each leg reciting—*Blessed Virgin Mary Mother of God make my legs well*—and he kisses the holy medal.

Rolling onto his tummy, Paddy rocks his head gently into the soft pillow thinking: *I'll be a sailor someday, too. Maybe even a ship's carpenter like Uncle Jack.*

Chapter X

The Hard Job Begins
January 24, 1941
Day: One Hundred and Twenty-three

"Ready for a ride, Champ?" Johnny Cant pushes the gurney up beside Paddy's bed.

"Where to?"

"You'll see."

Paddy puts the *Superman* comic aside. Johnny Cant slides off his covers and lifts him on to the gurney.

"Tell me where we're going, please," Paddy asks as they *clip-clop* from the room.

No answer.

Propped up on his elbows, Paddy watches anxiously as they reach Times Square and turn down Broadway—like they're going to the casting room. He flops back on the gurney.

"The casting room," he moans. "That's where we're going—to put them back on?"

"Nope," Johnny Cant says, grinning down at him.

They continue on, passing the casting room. Surprised, Paddy sits up, and there in an open doorway at the end of Broadway stands Ma Gillick.

"Well, Paddy, you finally made it," she says as they approach. "Welcome to my clinic."

"Hi!" Paddy says as the gurney sweeps past her into a large bright area.

Johnny Cant pushes the gurney next to a table along one side of the room. He moves Paddy on to its padded, black surface. Then, with a wink at him and a flash of gold teeth, he turns and *clip-clops* off.

"How are you?" Ma Gallic comes up beside the table.

"Great! No casts!" Paddy answers, dazed a little by the excitement.

"May I look at your legs?"

"Yes."

"Lie down. Let's see what we have to work with."

Settling back on the table, Paddy feels his gown go up to his hips and her hand touching the bent-up left knee. He squeezes the table as she presses down on it, very gently.

"Ouch," he groans, although she hardly hurt him.

"Botched job," Ma Gillick mumbles. She then slides her hand from his knee to his foot. Moving the foot up and down and side-to-side, she mumbles again, "Flaccid." With her other hand, she lightly squeezes Paddy's thigh.

"Some muscle tone here. That's good," she mumbles.

Walking around to the other side of the table, Ma Gillick asks, "What's your dad's job, Paddy?"

"Takes care of our apartment building. He's the super," Paddy answers, lifting his head to see what she is going to do next.

"Works hard, I bet." She moves his right foot up and down and side to side as she did with the left foot.

"Yes, he fixes everything, takes out all the garbage cans, puts coal into the furnace, and lots of stuff."

"Push your right foot down against my hand," she orders, holding the foot, toes pointed up.

He presses his foot against her hand.

"That's good. From now on, like your dad, you have a job."

"What's that?"

"Learning to walk again. And it will be a hard job. You up to it?"

"For sure!" he answers with a big grin while popping up on his elbows.

"Lie back and pull your right heel toward your seat."

"I can't," he responds, his mind spinning: *Walk again.*

"Do it. Lay back—pull your heel toward your seat," she repeats softly but sternly.

Paddy lowers himself to the table and tries to move his heel. It doesn't budge.

"See, I can't."

"I see nothing but a pouting face talking rubbish. *Can't*," she looks coolly at him, "we don't say *that word* around here. If I asked you to flap your arms and fly around my clinic, could you?"

"No," Paddy shakes his head.

"Right, it's not possible. That's an *I can't*. Nothing I ask you to do as part of your job here will be impossible and call for an *I can't* response from you. Many tasks, like pulling your heal toward your seat, will take a long time, a lot of work, and some pain to accomplish—but it will be accomplished. Understand?"

"Yes," he mumbles.

"So, rule one—*no I can'ts*. Don't want to hear that again. Now relax."

Sliding one hand under his right thigh, she lifts his leg a few inches off the table. He feels dull ache in his knee as it doesn't bend.

"That hurts," he moans.

"I know. Your legs are frozen stiff as boards from being so long in those casts."

"But you hurt me," he whimpers.

Looking at him, her face relaxed and kindly, she lowers his leg back to the table saying, "You know I'm here to help you?"

Paddy nods.

"But to help you, I must sometimes hurt you. That is the way it is."

She turns back to his leg, lifts it as before, with her hand under his thigh. He grips the sides of the table hard. She looks at him. Then, her eyes on his, she places her other hand on top of his lower leg and pushes gently down.

"Stop! Stop!" Paddy lifts his head screaming as the pain, like a violent electric shock, radiates through his leg.

"Paddy, look at me." Ma Gillick stops pushing and lowers his leg to the table.

"Yes," he snivels.

"When I hurt you bad," she says in a no-nonsense tone, "don't yelp. You say *hold please* instead—and you say it softly. I will then stop. That's rule number two—*no yelping*. You just say, *hold please.*"

"But..."

"No buts about it either. It is *hold please* when the pain is too much—and *no yelping.* That's rule two. *No yelping.* And what's rule one, Paddy?"

"I can't—*no I can'ts,*" he grumbles.

"Good. Now lie back."

Doing as he's told, Ma Gillick again lifts Paddy's right leg—and presses down.

"Stop!" He yells.

"Paddy." She stops pressing down but keeps the leg suspended above the table. "Rule two?"

"No yelping," he moans, tears trickling from his eyes.

"And what else?"

"Hold please."

Once more, she applies pressure gently down on his lower leg.

"Hold—hold please!" Paddy squeezes his eyes, gripping the table with all his might.

Ma Gillick stops and lowers the limb to the table, saying, "I know it hurts, Paddy. Still, we have to do it. Your legs are stiff from being so long in the casts. And before you can walk, we must to get rid of the stiffness. That will take some time."

"But it hurts really bad." He sobs, wiping his tears away with the back of his arm.

"Yes, I know. Now you must help bend the leg."

"Not again!"

"Once more. Work with me. As I press down, you try to bend it."

I can't wants to shout out from his mouth, but it doesn't.

She lifts the leg again and pushes down.

"Hold—hold—hold please!"

She releases the pressure and lowers the leg to the table.

"Did you try to bend your leg?"

"Yes," he lies.

"That's good, but that *hold please* was a bit loud—nearly a yelp."

"Sorry."

Paddy watches Ma Gillick then move around to the other side of the table, her eyes now on his left leg: *She's going to bend it, too!* A sour taste rises to his throat.

Resting her hand on the bent-up left knee, she looks at it for a moment shaking her head.

"We'll leave this one for next time." She smiles at him. "Okay?"

"Yes!" he says, swallowing the bad taste.

"We've made a good start, and we're almost done for today."

"What are you going to do now?" He sits up looking anxiously at her.

"Give you a massage. It won't hurt. Feels nice. I'll be right back."

Paddy watches as she walks toward a large cabinet near the clinic entrance. He then turns from her and looks around.

The clinic is a big room, like a gymnasium. Across the shiny wooden floor from him is a wall of windows—a basketball stand and lots of snow outside. In a neat row in front of the windows are two wheelchairs, four regular chairs, and three big, brown medicine balls. In the corner is a barrel with a bunch of crutches sticking out of it. Directly to his right are two more tables. Then there are pipes, like hand railings, coming out from the wall. On the wall between the railings is a tall mirror. Beyond that is a platform with stairs going up.

Ma Gillick returns carrying a towel and a jar, like a jam jar. She spreads the towel out under his legs, opens the jar, and scoops out a glob of greasy, tan colored cream.

"You were a very brave boy for me—very brave indeed." She smiles at him while rubbing the cream into her hands. "And I bet you remember the rules."

"*No I can'ts. No yelping*—just *hold please.*" He smiles back, and she begins softly massaging his limp left foot.

"That's good—excellent."

"What's that you're rubbing on me? Tickles."

"It's cocoa butter—makes the massaging easier, nicer." She moves her hand up to his bent knee and presses down very gently.

"Butter—like for toast?" He asks, griping the table and cringing as she presses slightly harder.

"No. Butter, like you put on toast, is made from cow's milk. Cocoa butter comes from a bean, the cocoa bean. The same bean from which chocolate is made."

"It's not brown like chocolate. Smells different, too," he says.

"That's because the seed of the cocoa bean is used to make chocolate. In making cocoa butter, only the oil in the bean is used. It's no Hershey bar," she smiles, "so don't try to eat it."

"Yuck!" Paddy laughs, thinking happily: Boy this part of my new job is nice—really nice.

CHAPTER XI

The Chariot, Swimming and Praying
February 4, 1941
Day: One Hundred and Thirty-four

"Something for ya, Champ."

"Holy cow—that's for me?"

"Yup! New transportation. Ya *chariot.*"

Johnny Cant rolls a wheelchair up to the bed, tossing a new *Superman* on Paddy's lap. He glances at the cover—Superman flying over a speeding train carrying a boy under his arm—and turns quickly back to the *chariot.*

"It's great. Help me get into it."

"Hold ya horses. Gotta fix the leg rests ta hold up them stiff legs of yours."

With the leg rests in position, sticking straight out from the seat, Johnny Cant removes Paddy's covers and lifts him into wheelchair.

"How's it feel?"

"Real good!" He smiles up at the giant while sliding his hands along the smooth wood armrests.

"Wicker back ain't tattered and the wheels run true as a dime, like new," Johnny Cant says. "And there's good brakes, too."

He squats beside Paddy and moves a break lever under the left armrest.

"See—one for each big wheel. Give 'em a try."

Paddy stretches over the high armrests, first to one side and then the other, moving the break levers back and forth.

"So what ya say? Ready ta try it out?"

"Yes!"

Johnny Cant whirls the *chariot* full circle, as Paddy laughs, and they roll out the door into the hallway.

"How about give'n me a hand. Push forward on them rings around the wheels. Here," he stops pushing, "like this, but watch out. Don't wanna run anyone down, if we can help it."

With his fingers just able to reach the rings, Paddy eagerly pushes as they continue along down the hallway.

"Ta get where ya go'n, ya gotta work now," Johnny Cant says teasingly. "No more free rides. You'll be missing my good old gurney."

"No I won't! Don't want to see that broken down thing again," Paddy huffs with a chuckle while trying his best to push the wheel rings.

They go their usual way, through Times Square and down Broadway toward Ma Gillick's clinic, with Paddy's heart racing with excitement: *Can't wait to show her my chariot!*

But before reaching the clinic entrance, they suddenly turn down a hallway that Paddy has never been down before.

"Stop! The clinic!" Paddy looks up at Johnny Cant.

"No, not today. Keep pushing."

"Where are we going? You never tell me."

"I do take'n and get'n, not tell'n—tell'n is what the docs and nurses does. Besides, today's a surprise."

"I don't like surprises!"

"Yeah—most is nasty but this one ain't."

"Honest?"

"Honest. Now push or we'll never get there."

"Tell me please."

"Push!" he orders.

Paddy returns to working the wheel rings, looking nervously ahead.

"Okay, ya can stop push'n," Johnny Cant says when they reach the end of the hallway. He then turns the *chariot* around and backs it through a door into a room. It's like a large bathroom with a long bench, towels stacked on the end of it.

"What's this?"

"It's the boy's dressing room for the swimming pool. Ya go'n for a swim."

"A swim! But I can't swim."

"Me neither, but you'll learn. Not me—too wet. Put the *chariot* brakes on."

Leaning over the armrests, Paddy shifts the leavers while watching Johnny Cant search through a tall locker.

"Here, let's get this on." He tosses a black swimsuit on to Paddy's lap.

Then, removing his hospital slippers and long nightshirt, he helps Paddy wiggle into the itchy wool trunks, hands him a towel, and backs the *chariot* through another door.

"Wow! It's big!" Paddy gasps, as Johnny Cant swings him around into the sun light streaming through large windows at the far end of the pool.

"Yeah, lots of water. Don't go roll'n yaself and the *chariot* in to it. Just wait." He secures the wheelchair brakes. "See ya later, Champ."

"You leaving me here alone?" Paddy asks nervously.

"I'll be back later."

"Okay—see you," Paddy answers, looking at all the sparkling water.

As Johnny Cant leaves, he then leans forward, trying to see the bottom of the pool while sniffing the chlorine smelling humid air.

Suddenly, a deep voice echoes across the water.

"So, yer Patrick—ur is it Paddy?"

Paddy looks up. A man in a swimsuit, with a black singlet top like his pop wears, is walking toward him along the side of the pool.

"Paddy!" His voice echoes back.

"My name's Mr. Cooney. I'm tae make a swimmer of you—what do you think of that?"

"Great!"

Mr. Cooney comes up to the *chariot* and crouches down.

"My pop was teaching me before I got sick," Paddy says eagerly.

"Aye, so you have a bit of a head start."

"I can duck under good and blow bubbles."

"Fine—noo, let's get yer wet."

"Okay." Paddy glances uneasily toward the water.

Standing, Mr. Cooney releases the *chariot's* brakes and wheels him to the side of the pool where there are stairs going down into the water. Next to the stairs lying on the pool deck is what looks like a cot, but without legs.

"You talk kind-a like my pop," Paddy says, as Mr. Cooney sets the *chariot* brakes.

"Aye? Whaur's he from?"

"Forest Hills."

"Nae, whaur was he born?" He steps over to the legless cot.

"Oh! Liverpool. That's in England."

"An' yer mum?"

"Ireland."

"An' yerself?"

"Forest Hills."

"Scotland, that's mah home. A wee town called Killing, on the end of Loch Tay. You know what a loch is?"

Paddy watches him fiddle with the cables that extend from each corner of the cot and attach to a rope that rises to ceiling.

"No." He shakes his head.

"In Scotland, lakes are called lochs." He pulls on a second rope coming down from the ceiling, and the cot rises a little from the deck.

"And Loch Tay is where ah learned tae swim—ice water, not hot like this bathtub." He lowers the cot and again squats beside Paddy. "What ah am gonnae do is sit you on this sling. Then, ah will pull you up some, swing you out from the deck, and lower you intae the water."

Paddy shakes his head, yes, feeling his heart pounding.

"Noo, before we get started, there's something you must never do." Mr. Cooney looks at him sternly. "Yer never are ter pee in the water."

"I won't."

"If you do—ah will know. The water, it will go green from a special chemical in it. Agreed?"

"Yes—I won't pee."

"Fine." Mr. Cooney stands and lifts Paddy from the *chariot* to the cot—*sling*. "Hold on, noo."

Paddy grips the sides of the sling rises while it swings out and lowers him into the water—feels cold, not hot like a bathtub. When the water is over Paddy's legs, Mr. Cooney secures the rope to a hook on the wall and splashes in beside him.

"Rest back." He places one hand on Paddy's back and the other under his seat. "Yer rigid as a board—loosen up, like yer takin' a nap. And keep yer legs on top of the water."

Mr. Cooney eases Paddy off the cot while he tries to keep his legs up—the right floats; the left sinks.

"We'll have tae take care of that." Mr. Cooney lifts the submerged leg and glides Paddy through the water on his back. "Yer don't want tae be draggin' an anchor about. Can you bend yer legs?"

"The right one, some. Not the left, yet. But we're working on that, me and Ma Gillick."

"Aye." He smiles.

As Paddy relaxes in Mr. Cooney's arms enjoying the rush of the water over his body, the thought jumps into his head: *I can sail the Britannia here.*

"Noo, take a hold of the gutter. Show me what yer dad taught you."

With Mr. Cooney holding him from behind, Paddy grasps the gutter on to the side of the pool and duck under blowing bubbles into the water.

"Good, laddie," he hears as his head rises and breaks the surface.

Then, while Paddy keeps hold of the gutter, Mr. Cooney raises his legs to the surface floating him on his stomach.

"Move yer legs—kick."

Struggling, rocking side-to-side, Paddy feels his right leg splashing a little. The left is still.

"The left leg, laddie—kick!"

He tries hard while Mr. Cooney moves the unresponsive leg up and down in the water.

"Okay fine. Duck-under—five times." Mr. Cooney releases Paddy's legs letting them sink.

"Now?"

"Aye—not tomorrer."

Paddy ducks under five times. Mr. Cooney then floats him around and around the pool on his back, releasing him now and then, but coming to the rescue before he begins to sink.

"Yer look a wee cold," Mr. Cooney says, gliding him to the pool stairs. "We'll stop...before you shrivel intae a prune."

Sitting side by side on the top step, towels over their shoulders and feet in the water, Mr. Cooney looks down at Paddy. "That's a bonnie medal you have there."

"Mom gave it to me." Paddy lifts the medal from his chest to show it. "It's got the *Blessed Virgin Mary* on one side and the *Sacred Heart of Jesus* on the other."

Mr. Cooney studies it a moment, and then he asks, "Do you know yer prayers?"

"Some. Mom just taught me a new one," he answers, letting the medal fall to his chest.

"Aye? Tell me."

While reciting the prayer—*Blessed Virgin Mary Mother of God make my legs well*—Paddy spots some shiny things at the bottom of the pool.

"What are they?" He points.

"Marbles—yer'ill soon be swimmin' down an' pickin' 'em up. Now, that's a fine prayer."

"I say it before I go to sleep and make the *Sign-of-the Cross* on my legs—like this." Paddy sketches crosses on his wet thighs. "And then I kiss the medal. Mom says it'll make me get better."

"O' aye."

"How many marbles are down there?"

"Hundred or so. Would you loch tae learn more prayers?"

"Sure—a hundred marbles?" The more Paddy looks the more of them he sees.

"At least. So then, at the end of each swim we'll spend a wee time learnin' yer prayers if ye loch. We'll start wi' the *Hail Mary.*" He reaches over placing Paddy's palms together in front of him.

"I know that. But not so good," Paddy says, scanning the pool bottom for more marbles.

"Weel, tae refresh yer memory, it goes like so:

Hail Mary, full of grace, the Lord is with thee,
blessed art though amongst women,
and blessed is the fruit of thy womb, Jesus.
Holy Mary, Mother of God,
Pray for us sinners now
and at the hour of our death.
Amen."

* * *

"What's the fruit of thy wound?" Paddy asks Nurse Edelstein that evening.

Nurse Edelstein is in a good mood, even listened without interrupting with lots of questions as he told her all about swimming. After his letters and numbers, she even read a story from the new *Superman*—like she's getting to like the comics.

"What's that?" She fluffs his pillow.

"Fruit of the wound."

"What on earth are you talking about?"

"The *Hail Mary.* Mr. Cooney is teaching me it. Gave me a *Holy Card,* too." He takes the *Holy Card* from his nightstand and hands it to her.

"Well, that's a nice picture, I guess." She momentarily studies the celestial figure: robed in pale blue, her chin raised, eyes rolled rapturously to the heavens.

"That's *The Blessed Virgin Mary* going to heaven. The *Hail Mary* words are on the back."

She turns the *Holy Card* over and reads the prayer to herself.

"Paddy," she says with a little laugh, "you have your words mixed up. It says fruit of thy *womb*. W-o-m-b—womb."

"Womb?"

"Yes, womb—w-o-m-b. Not wound—w-o-u-n-d." She shows him the card, pointing to the letters. "You spell womb—w-o-m-b."

"What's the womb?"

"That's the place inside a woman's belly, like a basket, where babies develop—where they grow until they're born. You'll learn about when you are older. The word fruit here," again she points to the *Holy Card*, "refers to the Jesus. He's the *fruit;* meaning the baby, growing in his mother's womb—*fruit of thy womb.*"

"Why do they call Jesus a fruit?" He takes back the *Holy Card* and look at the picture of the *Blessed Virgin Mary.* "And how did he get in the basket?"

"Ask Mr. Cooney—or is it *Father* Cooney now? It's a Catholic thing. And I'm not Catholic."

"You're not? How come?" He looks at her, surprised that not everyone is Catholic.

"No, I'm Jewish. Now go to sleep—but first, spell womb."

She points to the word on the *Holy Card.*

"W-o-m-b." Paddy reads the letters.

"And wound?"

"W-o-," he looks sadly at her. "Don't remember."

"W-o-u-n-d." She says the letters slowly.

"W-o-u-n-d." Paddy repeats them.

"Good. Remember the words. I'll ask again tomorrow. Good night."

Paddy watches her walk to the door and flip off the lights. Wiggling down under the cold covers, he says softly, "Blessed Virgin Mary Mother of God make my legs well," while making the *Signs-of-the-Cross* on his legs. And he kisses the holy medal.

Rolling over on his tummy, Paddy looks for a moment at the *Britannia* sitting on his nightstand in the moonlight, its long shadow stretching across the floor. Then, rocking his head into the pillow, he dozes off with happy thoughts: *Mr. Cooney. The great pool. All the colored marbles. And the terrific chariot—waiting for him by the door.*

CHAPTER XII

Blueberry Pie and Braces
February 10, 1941
Day: One Hundred and Forty

Ducking through the doorway, Johnny Cant asks, "What ya do'n?"

"Making a Valentine for my mom. Friday is Valentine's Day."

As he comes up beside the bed, Paddy holds up the valentine. Neatly printed above a partly colored heart is *TO MOM*, below the heart, *HAPPY VALENTINE'S DAY*, and then *LOVE, PADDY* under that.

"I drew heart and Nurse Kelly did the words. I'm coloring the heart red and the letters blue."

"Nice," Johnny Cant says. "But put it away. We're take'n a trip."

"Where?' Paddy grumbles placing the valentine and Crayolas on his night stand. "I know, you can't tell me."

Johnny Cant smiles, gold teeth shining. "Well, I shouldn't, but I will if ya don't let on."

"I won't. Promise."

"Friday may be Valentine's day, but today's get-measured-for-braces day."

"Wow! Ma Gillick said it would be soon—but already."

"Yup. Today's the day."

With Johnny Cant pushing some from behind, Paddy works the *chariot* wheel rings, which is easier now since Nurse Kelly put pillows on the seat raising him up to reach them better.

"Wanna go to the kitchen? See what's a-cook'n. Maybe even get us some pie," Johnny Cant asks as they cross Broadway and head down Throughway.

"We allowed to do that?"

"Ain't noth'n says we can't."

"But the braces?"

"We got time."

About halfway down Throughway, they shove the *chariot's* leg lifts against a large door with a round window and push it open into the kitchen.

"Miss Minnie, we're here!" Johnny Cant shouts. "'Bout die'n for a slice of ya wonderful pie!"

They wheel up to a long steel table with pots hanging over it. Paddy pushes himself in close to the table and puts on the brakes, while Johnny Cant slides a stool up beside it and sits down,

"Miss Minnie, we're here!" He shouts again.

"Hold ya horses," a scolding voice comes from behind a door at the far end of the kitchen. "I hear ya holler'n like some drunken preacher."

The door then swings open, and a colored woman in a long white apron walks toward them carrying a tray. She's slender and tall, almost as tall as Johnny Cant, with short, fuzzy black hair.

"Champ, this here lady's Miss Minnie," Johnny Cant says, grinning as she approaches. "And she's my Valentine. Ain't ya, Miss Minnie?"

"Be a cold day in hell when I'm ya Valentine, Johnny Cant." She comes up close beside him and places the tray on the table, looking down at Paddy. "Now this handsome gent, he could be my Valentine. But be'n called *Champ*," she shakes her head, "I don't know. That ain't no name. What's ya real name, boy?"

"Paddy," he answers, gazing hungrily at the two large slices of pie and big glasses of milk waiting on the tray.

"Paddy, well that's more like it. That's blueberry pie ya gape'n at, child. Help yaself."

"He's got himself a Valentine already, his mom," Johnny Cant says, taking two forks, the pies, and milks from the tray and placing them on the table. "Made her a card, too. But ya consider yaself a lucky woman. Miss. Minnie—ya got me."

"Dream on, Johnny Cant—dream on. What I got is work ta do. Now eat up and get outta here," she says, nudging Johnny Cant with her hip as she walks off.

"Beautiful, ain't she?" Johnny Cant sighs, watching her move quickly away.

"Yes," Paddy mumbles, gobbling his pie.

* * *

After some twists and turns, they enter a short, dimly lit hallway with garbage cans and cardboard boxes stacked along one wall.

"This looks like my pop's basement," Paddy says cautiously. "Smells bad like it, too."

Johnny Cant steers the *chariot* through an open door into a room, as poorly lit as the hallway, and crowded with machines and cluttered work benches. The odor is pleasant, leather and glue.

"Hi, Paddy," Ma Gillick's voice rings out.

As his eyes adjust, he sees her standing off to one side of the room. Beside her is a man, a head shorter than her, wearing a leather apron that hangs down to his shoes. On his head is a strange white hat that's with no brim.

"Hi!" Paddy pushes the wheelchair over to them.

"This is Mr. Lombardi." Ma Gillick introduces the little man.

Mr. Lombardi nods, his mouth turned down as if he's angry at someone.

"Hello," Paddy says, applying the *chariot* brakes.

"Mr. Lombardi is going to make your braces," says Ma Gillick with a big smile.

"Thank you," Paddy replies politely, while looking more closely at Mr. Lombardi's strange hat, thinking: *Kind-a like priests have on going to the altar to say mass,*

He gets another stern nod from the brace maker.

Johnny Cant then lifts Paddy from the *chariot* and sits him, legs extended, on a long, narrow wooden table that extends out from the wall.

"Let's take off your slippers and trousers," says Ma Gillick, as Mr. Lombardi clicks on a light hanging above the table.

Paddy now sees the hat clearer: *It's made of newspaper.*

When Ma Gillick finishes undressing Paddy, Mr. Lombardi places a large brown paper bag and a tape measure on the table. He looks at Paddy's naked feet and legs for a long moment and then gently wiggles the floppy left foot. Next, he measures the foot from heal to toe, takes a stubby pencil from behind his ear, licks the tip, and scratches lines and numbers on the brown paper bag.

Ma Gillick, peering over Mr. Lombardi's shoulder, mumbles something. He glances up at her emitting a barely audible growl. She steps away and moves off to the side to stand quietly next to Johnny Cant.

The little brace maker continues measuring Paddy's feet and legs with quick, sure movements—up, down, and around—and drawing lines and scratching numbers on the paper bag. Finally, he stops, returns the stubby pencil to his ear, and for a long time looks back and forth from Paddy's legs to the paper bag checking his work. Following a grunt and nod, he then neatly folds the paper bag, and, along with the tape measure, slides it into his apron pocket.

CHAPTER XIII

First Steps
March 31, 1941
Day: One Hundred and Eighty-nine

The days are all much the same now. Weekday mornings, it's Ma Gillick's clinic or to swimming. Swimming is Paddy's favorite thing. He can now float on his back and stomach, dogpaddle, and pick marbles from the bottom of the pool with his right toes but not with the *feeble* left ones.

After lunch, he does puzzles Nurse Edelstein gave him, colors in the *Red Ryder* coloring book, swings the red and silver magnet, and looks at comic books. There is also homework: letters and numbers for Nurse Edelstein and exercises for Ma Gillick, which Nurse Kelly helps him with. Sometimes, Johnny Cant takes him to the boring solarium or for brace fittings with grumpy Mr. Lombardi.

Going to the brace shop is fun, though. They always stop to see Miss Minnie to get pie. Johnny Cant likes her—a lot! And yesterday he discovered that she *really likes* him. When they stopped at the kitchen, Miss Minnie brought the milk and pie like always. Johnny Cant gulped his down faster than usual. He then followed her through the door at the back of the kitchen, which he had never done before.

He was gone for a long time. So, having finished his treat, Paddy pushed the *chariot* to the door, opened it a little, and peeked in to see them—hugging and kissing. Spinning the *chariot* around, he hightailed it back to the table. They didn't see him.

Later, when he told Nurse Kelly about the *hugging and kissing*—he tells her everything—she laughed so hard her face turned red as her hair while torrent of tears streamed down her cheeks. She then made Paddy promise, crossing his heart, not to tell anyone else, especially not Nurse Edelstein.

During the day, Paddy talks a lot with Nurse Kelly, who likes to reminisce about her home and friends in Ireland. He also talks some to Johnny Cant when they go places, but Johnny Cant says very little. At the clinic, he and Ma Gillick talk mostly about his treatments while she helps him do *his job*. At the pool, Mr. Cooney likes to explain things about his swimming and to teach him his prayers; he knows the *Hail Mary* and the *Our Father* by heart and learning the *Apostles' Creed,* about Jesus being crucified. The few children he sees are *the big kids* passing in the hallways—they never say anything to him.

After supper, Paddy goes over his homework with Nurse Edelstein and does his lessons. He can add and subtract a little and read, without much help, from *Little Toot*—about a tugboat that learns not to be afraid of the ocean. Also, Nurse Edelstein is reading *Alice's Adventures in Wonderland* to him. And, if he does extra good with his lessons, she will read some from one of his *Superman* comics. Johnny Cant has so far given him four. .

On weekends, there's no clinic, no swimming, no nothing, just a weekend nurse and someone bringing the food tray—always different people. Paddy spends the time then playing in his room or going up and down Throughway in the *chariot*—going beyond his hallway is *out of bounds.* That's Nurse Kelly's rule.

Also, he watches the squirrels. They're back, running up and down the big tree—there's a baby squirrel now, too. Otherwise, weekends are very quiet. And often he gets sad, hoping his Mom and Pop will visit. They don't anymore.

* * *

Rolling the *chariot* through the clinic door, Johnny Cant walking behind him, Paddy calls to Ma Gillick, "I pushed all the way here by myself."

"That's very good, Paddy—but guess what?" She smiles as he wheels up to the exercise table where she is waiting for him.

"What?"

"The braces, they're done."

"Oh boy! When do I get them?"

"Mr. Lombardi will be here with them soon. So, let's get started."

Johnny Cant lifts him from the *chariot* to the table and leaves, as always. They then do the bending, pushing, and stretching. The right leg bends—*flexes*—and it straightens— *extends*—almost all the way. Ma Gillick is teaching him the *technical* words. The left leg *flexes* only a little, and the striking pain still comes when Ma Gillick pushes down on the knee to try and straighten it. Also, the left foot still just flops around—*flaccid.*

While Ma Gillick is manipulating the *flaccid* foot, Mr. Lombardi rushes into the clinic carrying the braces. At the table, he grunts at Ma Gillick and nods to Paddy—

his usual greetings. But, today, he seems different. Then Paddy sees it—his square hat has colors.

Seeing Paddy staring, Mr. Lombardi flicks paper with his finger. "Made from the Sunday funnies—for special occasion," he mutters, placing the braces on the table.

"Wow!" Paddy shouts cheerfully, more in response to Mr. Lombardy actually saying something than to the new newspaper hat.

"Well, Paddy, shall we put them on?" Ma Gillick says, reaching for the braces.

"Yes!"

Mr. Lombardi slides the brace away from Ma Gillick's hand. Half smiling at him, she steps a little back from the table.

Mr. Lombardi then quickly puts *fitting socks* on Paddy, slides the braces up on to his legs, glides his feet into the attached *boots,* and straps the brace bars to his legs: one thick strap below the knee, three thin ones securing a lather *knee cap,* and two more thick straps at the top of his thigh. Lastly, he laces and ties the *boots.*

"They feel okay, Paddy?" Ma Gillick asks moving back beside the table.

"Great—real good!" he lies. They're stiff and tight, almost like the not forgotten casts.

"Fine," Ma Gillick comes back close to the table, "now you're ready to walk."

"I can't!" he blurts out, struck with a jolt of panic.

"Hey—the rule," Ma Gillick says softly, feigning a stern look.

"No *I can'ts,*" he mumbles.

"Okay, let's do it."

Taking Paddy under the arms, she slides him from the table; his legs starting to tremble as soon as the brace boots touch the floor.

"Relax, Paddy. Grasp the table with your right hand. I won't let you fall," Ma Gillick says softly.

As he does so, she turns him to face the end of the table while stepping behind him and taking hold of his waist.

"Now, we'll walk to the end of the table. I'll help move the left leg. You can move the right on your own."

Paddy looks back at her with a doubtful expression.

"Go ahead. You can do it. Right leg first," she orders.

He slides his right leg forward.

"That's not so hard." He smiles down at the leg.

"Okay. I'll now slide the left leg forward and then you move the right leg forward again."

In this way, tilting side to side from brace to brace, Paddy moves down the table with Ma Gillick counting each step.

"That's one—and two—and three—and four."

At the end of the table, they pause, rest a second, turn, and go on across the end.

"One—two—and three." The steel braces getting heavier and heavier as if turning to lead.

They pause again, turn, and continue down the other side of the table.

"One—two—three—and four—*and five!*"

Ma Gillick moves him around to face the table. "Fine. Far enough for today. That was wonderful. Eleven steps!"

Standing directly across from Paddy is Mr. Lombardi, his head down studying the lines and numbers on the brown paper bag spread out on the table. Slowly the brace maker looks up, his face morphing from grouch to grin.

"Bravo, piccino—bravo," he says, reaching over and patting Paddy's hand. "The braces—okay?"

"They're great. Real good," he answers, breathing heavy.

Then all at once, Paddy's throat tightens. His entire body starts shaking. And a torrent of tears burst from his eyes rolling in great drops down his cheeks.

"Paddy, what's the matter?" Ma Gillick wraps her arm around his shoulder pulling his close to her.

"I-don't-know." he gasps, his chest heaving. "I like the braces—a really lot."

With a gentle hug, she softly kisses his forehead. "A little too much excitement. But you did very well, Paddy. I'm so proud of you."

* * *

"Tell me all about it—*again*—some other time," Johnny Cant says, leaving Paddy at Time Square to make his own way back to his room. "Ya can go the rest of the way on your own. Gotta go."

"Okay. Bye." Paddy waves and heads down Throughway, pushing the *chariot* as fast as he can toward his room.

"Sure, watch where yer goin'," Nurse Kelly shouts, jumping aside as he races through his open door.

"Got the braces! I walked them! I did great!"

"I'm sure you did, *Mr. Wonderful*," she says, looking at his legs as he spins the *chariot* around in circles. "An' where are the glorious devices?"

"I can't keep them—not yet—Mr. Lombardi, he has to do adjustments. Ma Gillick says I got to practice more in them. But I walked all around the table by myself and..."

* * *

Later Mr. Martin enters the room delivering the dinner tray. Paddy, alone now, is lying on his stomach watching the squirrels scratching at the grass around the tree. He quickly rolls over sitting up in his bed and calls out excitedly, "Mr. Martin, I got braces!"

Mr. Martin rests the tray on his lap while Paddy starts telling him about how good he walked around the table all by himself.

With his gummy smile, Mr. Martin interrupts him. "Hold on kid-o."

Bending over, he slides up his pant legs, straightens up, and gives Paddy a big, gummy smile. "Ya ain't the only one. See, got braces, too!"

Paddy looks in amazement thinking: *they're like mine—just like them.*

Mr. Marten then moves back from the bed and standing at attention, tilted a little to one side, he chants softly:

We're aces,
Got brace-is,
Steel rods,
Buckle straps,
High boots—
Wi' crisscrossin',
Crisscrossin',
Crisscrossin' lace-is.

With that, he turns in a circle, snapping his fingers over his head, performing a wobbly, stiff-leg dance.

They're both laughing like crazy when Nurse Edelstein comes in to the room. Mr. Martin looks at her, quickly lowers his pant legs, and heads for the door, reciting under his breath: "We're aces, Got brace-is..."

"Hay, Nurse Edelstein!" Paddy hollers out. "I got them. The braces. And I walked all around the table..."

CHAPTER XIV

The Red Tricycle and Letter from Pop
July 1, 1941
Day: Two Hundred and Eighty

Still don't look like real walking, Paddy is thinking as he watches his image reflected in the mirror at the end of the parallel bars. His body still tilts to one side while swinging the left leg forward, but much less since Mr. Lombardi fixed the brace to bend some at the knee. He also shortened the right brace. It now goes only up to his knee. And Paddy's getting stronger. Yesterday he walked *solo*—no crutches, no cane, no Ma Gillick—all the way around the perimeter of the clinic.

"Now the stairs," Ma Gillick calls over to him.

"Okay."

He totters over to the stairs and pauses looking up at the platform. Climbing up, that's the hardest. Holding the railing with one hand, he raises his short brace leg up on to the first step. Then, pulling on the railing, he straightens the leg and drags the long brace leg up behind. When the long brace is set on the step, he steps up again with the short brace leg. He does this—step and drag—seven times to get to the platform.

Going down, he faces the railing. Holding it with both hands, he lowers the long brace leg to the step below and then hops the short brace leg down beside it. Lowering and hopping, he gets himself to the bottom of the stairs.

"That'll do, Paddy. Come, sit down here," Ma Gillick gestures to him. She's standing by a chair in the middle of the floor.

"I only went up and down once. Got four to go," he answers.

"Enough for now. Come over here and sit down"

He makes his way to the chair and plops into it.

"Close your eyes," she says.

"Why?" He looks up at her.

"Just close your eyes. Cover them with your hands. No peeking."

"Why?"

"Trust me. Do it."

He does as he's told, listening to his heart beating in his ears. Then, whispering—footsteps—more whispering—quiet again. He wants to peek, badly.

"Okay, Paddy, open your eyes," Ma Gillick finally says.

He pulls his hands away.

"Holy Cow!" he gasps

Before him is a tricycle, red like the one at home—but shiny, new. He looks up at Ma Gillick. Next to her, giving him a thumbs-up is Johnny Cant. Mr. Lombardi is standing behind him, looking grouchy as usual.

"Well, don't just gape at it," Ma Gillick says. "You want to take a ride or do I return it to the store."

"Yes, I want to!" Paddy smiles, pushing himself up from the chair

With Ma Gillick assisting, he climbs on to the tricycle. Mr. Lombardi then attaches a strap to the left pedal and buckles it over my *flaccid* foot.

"Dat 'ill hold it in place," he mumbles.

With Ma Gillick helping from behind, Paddy pedals off around the clinic.

"Can I ride it back to my room?" he asks excitedly as they return to the chair.

"Not yet. Your legs have to get stronger for that."

He goes around the clinic once more by himself calling to his audience, "It's super. I mean, real super!"

* * *

Sprawled out on his stomach, head at the end of the empty bed, Paddy keeps looking up from his coloring—a picture of Red Ryder's Indian pal Little Beaver and his horse Papoose—waiting for Nurse Kelly to tell her about the new tricycle.

At last, she rushes into the room. "An' haven't I something for you," she says.

"I got a tricycle." He rolls over and sits up.

"Never mind that for now. You got yerself a letter."

"A letter—for me?"

"Who else? Has yer name on the envelope. But maybe I better check to be sure it's not for another," she says, pretending to leave.

"No! It's me. I know it is."

She pulls the letter from her pocket and sits beside him on the bed.

"Let's see." She holds up the envelope. "The return address is 452 Yates Street, Albany, New York. Who do you know in Albany?"

"Albany—where's that?" He snatches the envelope from her hand.

"It's Upstate. Open it. See who it's from."

Tearing the envelope apart, he removes two folded pages and opens them.

"You read it." He offers Nurse Kelly the pages.

"You read it. Be good practice."

"No, it'll take forever. You do it—*please*."

Taking the letter, she looks at it for a second.

"'Tis from your dad. Nice handwritin'—firm and clear."

"Gosh, from Pop! Go on, read it! Read it!"

Sliding up on to the bed, she begins Paddy's first letter, ever. It went something like this:

18 June 1941

Dear Son,

I hope you are doing ok. I am sorry for not visiting you for so long. It has been a busy time. But I have some good news. First off, you have a brother now. Born 5 March. Billy is his name, after me. He is a happy little chap.

And I have a new job. I am a handyman at the college here in Albany. We moved last month into the bottom floor of a house. The place needs some fixing but will do. Mrs. Beck who owns the house lives upstairs with seven cats.

Your sister Kate is here with us but not Patsy and Betty. With the new baby, the move, your mum's nerves, and all, we could not keep them. Your Aunt Margaret said she could not either. So, they are now in Saint Joseph's Home run by the nuns. It is near Fishkill. Not far from where you're at. We will get them back when things improve.

Your mom is here beside me as I write. She says to tell you the Valentine card arrived just a few days ago. It went to Forrest Hills and had to be forwarded to us in Albany. It is lovely, she says, and it is up on the icebox. Now Kate wants to write something.

Hi Paddy,

Albany is nice. You will like it. There is a park nearby and so is my school. I am really looking forward to it starting and I can have some friends. That is still five weeks from now.

It is different now without Patsy and Betty. But there is little Billy and he's so cute. He smiles all the time—but he is very stinky, too, sometimes. Yuck! Just kidding. You will like him a lot.

I miss you.

Love, Kate XXXooo

That is it for now, son. When we are all settled, your mam and I will be down to see you. It will be a while though as I am very busy learning the ropes here. Anyway, you will be home soon. Your mom sends hr love.

Your Father.

Nurse Kelly folds the pages and hands them to Paddy. "Is that all?" He stares at them.

"Yes. And a brilliant letter, with your sister writing some as well."

Placing the letter into the battered envelope, he moans, "But they won't come see me."

"Your mother's not well. An' there's the new baby—your dad's new job," Nurse Kelly says softly. "Now don't go gettin' all teary-eyed on me. Here, let me get your colorin' book."

"No," he whimpers, "read *Superman*—the one on my nightstand."

"Oooo, sure, I will. Who could resist the likes of 'em—them blue britches an' 'al?" She laughs, bouncing from the empty bed to get the comic book.

* * *

"Hello." A new nurse hurries into the room.

"Hi!" Paddy answers, looking up at her.

He's still lying on the empty bed where he has been waiting impatiently for Nurse Edelstein to arrive so he can show her the letter.

"Where's Nurse Edelstein?" he asks.

"Night off," she answers, turning the covers down on his bed. "Come now, over here. Time for bed."

"I go to the bathroom first."

"Yes, of course. I'll take you." She moves quickly toward the *chariot*.

"No, I do that myself."

"Okay, fine. I'll be back."

After the bathroom, Paddy's is in his own bed, the nurse dashes back into the room.

She comes to a stop just inside the doorway and places her hands on her hips. "You're already in bed. I'm supposed to help you," she says, flustered. "Well, what's done is done."

"I got a letter..." Paddy says.

"Good night." She turns away from him, flips off the light, she disappears into the hallway.

Making the *Sign-of-the-Cross* on his legs, Paddy whispers Mom's prayer and then kisses the holy medal. Rolling on his stomach, he retrieves the battered envelope from under his pillow and removes the pages. Turning them to the moon lit window, he slowly works his way through the words, reading some and remembering the rest. He then places the letter on his nightstand, and rocking his head gently into the pillow, he drifts off into a dream:

He's flying fast behind the jalopy.
Getting close now.

Faces suddenly appear in the rear window—Patsy and Betty, crying.
He flies faster! Faster!
Their lips are moving—hurry! Hurry! Hurry!
Wait! Wait! Wait! He shouts—the words coming with no sound.
Faster! Flying faster!
The jalopy races into a tunnel
The tunnel vanishes!
A mountain—he's going to hit it!
Pulling up on the flying stick!
Pulling hard!
Up! Up! Up!
Feeling the warm flow between his legs.

Paddy jerks awake. He stays still listing to a branch of the big tree softly tapping the window as the dream fades. He then removes his nightgown, drops it on the floor. Wiggling from wet, he slides down under the covers pulling them over his head.

CHAPTER XV

Mr. Bones and Shm-ha-in Ghosts
October 30, 1941
Day: Four Hundred and One

Two squirrels, an adult and the baby, are sitting at the bottom of the big tree breaking open nuts and eating the inside. One is missing. As Paddy leans over the handle bars of his tricycle to look up the tree for the third squirrel, a loud *thump-thump-thump* comes from behind him. The squirrels freeze. Paddy about leaps from the tricycle seat.

Again, louder—*thump-thump-thump*—as if someone is kicking his door. He swings the tricycle about and looks to the open doorway. No one's there. He pedals forward hearing a clattering coming from the hallway, like sticks hitting together. He pauses and continues very slowly—more clattering.

Suddenly, with a thunderous *Boo*, a wiggling skeleton jumps into the doorway—stopping Paddy dead in his tracks.

"Scared ya, didn't I?" Johnny Cant laughs, ducking into the room holding up the skeleton by a hook coming from the top of its head.

PATRICK J. BIRD

"No, you didn't," Paddy stammers, feeling his heart pounding away. "Who'd be scared of some fake old skeleton?"

"You! That's who! And he ain't no fake. Mr. Bones here, he's the genuine article." Johnny Cant extends the skeleton's bony hand towards Paddy. "Mr. Bones, this here's Champ. Champ, Mr. Bones. Well, ya gonna shake, or what?"

Smiling warily, Paddy reaches from the tricycle and touches the tips of the bony fingers. "Hi, Mr. Bones."

"Mr. Bones, he's come ta celebrate Halloween with ya—keep ya company." Johnny Cant slips the skeleton's head hook over one of the ceiling pipes.

"Halloween?" Paddy says, staring at Mr. Bones dangling in the middle of the room.

"Yup. Tonight's when there's ghosts, goblins—all dem creepy things come 'round."

"Where did you get it...Mr. Bones?" He pedals up closer to the skeleton and slides his hand down its leg, feels soapy.

"From the doc's conference room."

"You just, just took it?"

"Borrowed, not took."

"Won't you get in trouble?"

"Nah. Won't be missed. Got-a-go now. Take good care of Mr. Bones."

Johnny Cant turns and rushes out the door, nearly bumping into Nurse Kelly coming into the room.

"Sorry, ma'am," he says with a little bow.

"No harm done," she answers, her eyes focused on Mr. Bones.

Crossing the room, Nurse Kelly circles the skeleton, looking it carefully up and down as if it was some special item for sale.

112

"Well, well, isn't this a sight now?"

"It's Mr. Bones," Paddy says coolly.

"Mr. Bones is it? Spittin' image of Martin Flynn, he is. himself to a tee—good-natured grin an' al'. Though a few stones lighter."

She gives Mr. Bones a little shove. The skeleton clatters softly.

"Martin Flynn? Who's that?" Paddy asks.

"An old flame from back in Belmullet." She pulls open the skeleton's spring- loaded jaw and lets it snap shut. "Where'd it come from?"

"Johnny Cant borrowed him from the doctor's conference room."

"Oh, he did, did he? He'll have the devil to pay for that." She lifts the skeleton's arm and curiously examines its bony hand.

"But it's Halloween," Paddy says, hoping maybe that's an excuse for Johnny Cant.

"Sure, don't I know that?" She drops the arm and pushes him again, but harder. Mr. Bones does a little clattering dance.

"Ah, well, pleased ter meet you Mr. Bones." She smiles at the skeleton while executing a slight curtsey.

"And now, Paddy," she turns to him, "we best get on with your exercise homework or we'll have Ma Gillick down on us."

Helping him from the tricycle and on to his bed, she remarks, "You know Halloween began in Ireland?"

"It did?" Paddy scoots back on the bed, his braced legs stretched out before him.

"O' indeed." Nurse Kelly begins unbuckling the brace straps. "That was far back in history, though. Back when we Irish were a bunch of 'eathens."

"What's an 'eathens?" he asks, helping with the top straps.

"'Eathens—them that worship rocks, an' trees, an' anything else that grabs their fancy. Of course, that was all before St. Patrick brought Christianity to Ireland."

"You mean that Halloween started in Ireland, really—ghosts and stuff?"

"Oooo, indeed!" She says and starts unlacing his boots. "As 'eathens, you see, the Irish believed that on the night before Halloween—*Shm-ha-in* they called it—the divide between the livin' an' the dead disappeared into no more than a fog. An' through the fog the dear departed—an' them not so dear—would drift back to earth."

"Wow! What would they do, hurt you—like eat you?"

"They could I'm sure, But most did no harm a' tall." She slips off the boot, sliding the braces from his legs. "They'd just drift about, here an' there, seein' what's happenin'. You might catch a glimpse of one—a milky haze floatin' past a doorway. That could scare you a bit. But some, well they held grudges."

"Grudges, what's that?"

"The feelin' of ill will. Anger against a person, or an entire clan, for doin' 'em wrong—like stealin' money or property or not showin' proper respect, or sure who knows what. Could be any slight really."

"What would they do—the ghosts, the angry ones?"

"Cause a barrel of mischief." She removes his socks. "Pull down fences, chase animals to exhaustion, an' scare the bejaysus out of man, woman, an' child."

"Could you chase them away?"

"Of course not—they're dead. They fear nothin'. Do as they please, they do," she says gravely while removing his trousers.

"You believe in ghosts? I mean *really* believe?"

"Didn't once. I do now, though."

"Why?"

"Scared not to."

"Why?"

"Sure, yer full of questions? An' we have to get on with the exercises."

"Tell me why, please, why you believe in them now and didn't."

"Ah' well," she sighs. "I'm forever spoilin' yer. We'll say we've finished exercises, you get enough of 'im, an' skip to the massage while I tell you."

"Thanks." He smiles, sitting up tall ready for a good story.

Nurse Kelly gets the jar of cocoa butter from the cabinet under his nightstand, opens the lid, and scoops out a glob of the brownish cream

"You see," she says, rubbing the cream into her hands, "when I was a young girl, a story teller, Mary Ford was her name, would on occasion visit our cottage to tell of Ireland's many mysteries an' grand wonders. Great fun, it was—but for this one Halloween eve."

Paddy rests back in the bed, feeling her soft hands gliding over his left leg and its *flaccid* foot.

"That night, we're all gathered 'round the turf fire— mother, father, me sisters Catherine an' Nora, an' brothers Gary, Martin, an' Sean. The whole brood.

"An' there I am, but a few years older than you are now, sprawled on the floor at mother's feet close to the fire listen' to Mary Ford tellin' of people goin' through the field just across the road from our place an' there bein' lost for days. An' of horses left in that very same field at sundown to be found in the mornin', covered with sweat—lookin' as if they'd been chased 'round all night.

"'*Tis the work of Shm-ha-in ghosts,* she's sayin' with that weighty tone of hers. Now, bein' bored, as I was with about everything then, I interrupt her, which you see is never ever done! *Mrs. Ford,* I say, I don't believe in *Shm-ha-in ghosts*—or ghosts of any kind. I've never seen even one in me entire life.

"Well, it was as if I'd pulled the heavens down on us. Mary Ford's dark eyes are on me in a flash—sending such a cold shiver all through me. Oh, the dreadful look, Paddy. I'll never forget it—could split stone, it could!

"An' mother, she's up an' on her feet in an instant—her face white as chalk. 'Child!' she said, yer'ill be bringin' a ton av bad luck down upon this house with such talk.' I could feel the fear in her voice. Pullin' me up then by me ear, she scoots me off to bed—with a good, solid whack on the rump.

"Well now," Nurse Kelly moves her supple hands to his right leg, "the next mornin', Mother, busy gettin' us all off to school, says nothin' to me—not even so much as a good mornin'. I throw down me breakfast, an' like the mouse fleein' the cat, I'm out the door.

"Outside, a soft rain is fallin'. So, instead of takin' the road to school, I decide on a shortcut through the field—the very one Mary Ford was tellin' about—thinking nothin' of it as I'd crossed the field a hundred times before."

She pauses and gently squeezes Paddy's right thigh.

"That tickles," he squawks as his right leg tightens reflexively.

"Yer getting' some real muscle here," she squeezes again.

"Stop! Please, go on with the story."

She resumes the massaging and continues.

"So down the hill I run, then over the road, and through the gate into the field. An' soon as I'm but a few strides into the field, doesn't this gray fog rise up before me. I stop right away, of course—as I had not seen such a strange thing before—an' turn back for the gate. But, instead of comin' to the gate, I find meself lost in the fog. And I knew the field like the back of me hand.

"Now, there I am, goin' around an' around not findin' me way when suddenly didn't it come to me—'tis the work of *Shm-ha-in ghosts.* Ooo, the thought gave me such a terrible fright I couldn't move. Then it came to me, what Mary Ford once told us: *Should ever encounter a Shm-ha-in ghost,* she said, *there's but one thing to do: You must at once turn al' your pocket inside out—bein' sure not to miss one. An' you then spin 'round three times, no more or no less, clappin' your hands over your head.*

"Droppin' me books, I hurriedly pull all me pockets inside out. The two in me skirt went fine. But the one in me blouse, it was sewed in. Still, I pull hard at it several times in hopes that would do. An' I spin 'round three times, no more or no less, clappin' me hands over me head.

"An' sure enough, didn't the gray fog lift—an' there, right before me, is the gate from the field. Gatherin' up me books, I race through the gate and down the road to town—faster I hoped than any *Shm-ha-in* ghost could chase me. Well, as I run up to the schoolhouse, the bell of Holy Trinity Church was striking. It was not the eight strokes I would be expectin'—but twelve times the bell struck. I couldn't believe me ears! It was noon! I'd been goin' around an' around the field for hours; yet, it seemed no more than minutes."

Nurse Kelly stops her massaging and takes a towel from the cabinet under Paddy's nightstand.

"Wow," Paddy utters softly, resting back on his elbows, "But why did they want to scare you or something—the *Shm-ha-in ghosts*?"

"For sayin' I didn't believe in them—or ghosts of any kind. What else? A small slight, to be sure. But you see many of the ghosts crossin' the divide on the night of *Shm-ha-in* have been dead hundreds of years, or more. Still, grudges are eatin' at them, festerin' away. An' being dead so long, they can find no one alive that did 'em wrong. So, in their frustration, they're quick to take offense at the slightest twit—from any living soul."

While cleaning cocoa butter from his legs with the towel, she leans toward him whispering, as if an angry *Shm-ha-in* ghost might be listening, "You must always be mighty careful, Paddy, with what her say about things you don't understand."

"It all really happened? I mean, really?" Paddy whispers back.

"May lightnin' strike me twice if it didn't," she answers brightly while straightening up and wiping the cocoa butter from her hands. "Life's full of queer things— *Shm-ha-in ghosts* bein' not the least of 'em."

* * *

Nurse Edelstein rushes into the room soon after Nurse Kelly has gone off duty. She glairs momentarily at Paddy, her eyes wide and lower lip turned down, and then detaches Mr. Bones from the ceiling pipe. Holding him up by his head hook, she hurries off, the skeleton clattering along beside her.

She's soon back. Saying nothing about Mr. Bones, they get right to the lessons, with Nurse Edelstein quick to scold Paddy for the slightest error. Then, with no story, she leaves, turning off the light—no good night either.

He wanted to tell her about the *Shm-ha-in* ghosts. But he's glad he didn't, thinking: *She would say it's not true and maybe be mad at Nurse Kelly, too.*

He told Mr. Martin at supper, though. That was after he almost fell down laughing about Johnny Cant borrowing Mr. Bones. And Mr. Martin said ghosts are real, "for sure". Then with his gummy grin, he recited a comical rhyme:

Mess wi' ghosts,
Ya're toast,
Worst yet,
A blackened roast.

And he hastily limped from the room; again laughing as he gave Mr. Bones such a big shove the skeleton hook almost rattled free from the ceiling pipe.

After Nurse Edelstein leaves, Paddy makes the *Sign-of-the-Cross* on his legs—adding to his mom's prayer: *please don't let Nurse Edelstein get Johnny Cant in trouble about Mr. Bones.* He kisses the holy medal, turns on his tummy rocking his head into dreamland:

Cotton clouds drift lazily below forming pictures:
A long eared rabbit,
A sitting dog,
A fat face yawning,
And a skull.
He pulls up on flying stick, going higher watching the skull take shape:
The hollow eyes, the snapping jaw, the hook—rising from its head.
He pulls up harder, soaring higher.
The hook is reaching up—up for him!
Higher, faster he climbs.
The hook chases after him—reaching, reaching.

It seizes the stick—pulls—snatching it away!
He's falling, falling.
Elation! Terror!
Heart hammering in his chest—head screaming!
Mommy! Mommy! Mommy!

"Child, wake up," Nurse Edelstein is saying softly as Paddy opens his eyes, feeling wetness under him.

"I peed," he moans.

"Indeed, you did. You're soaked through," she says, standing beside the bed.

"I'm sorry. I had a bad dream."

"What about?" She slides down his covers.

"Mr. Bones becoming a ghost."

"A skeleton becoming a ghost? Now that's a new one. But I guess appropriate for Halloween. Tell me about it."

"I can't remember. It's gone."

"Just as well."

She helps him off with his gown and then strips away the soggy blankets and sheets.

"You mad at me?" he asks, wiggling into a fresh garment.

"No. But you must control yourself—no more wetting the bed."

"Are you going to tell on Johnny Cant?"

"He did a bad thing, but I won't tell on him. The skeleton is back where it belongs." She smiles and pats his head. "Mr. Bones wasn't missed."

She then quick remakes his bed, gathers up the soggy blankets and linens, and heads for the door.

"Good night, Paddy. No more dreams or wet beds." Nurse Edelstein flips off the light as she steps into the hallway.

Paddy slides down between the cool, fresh sheets and warm, clean blankets, a smile on his face, thinking: *Johnny Cant, he said Mr. Bones wouldn't be missed.*

He kisses the holy medal, muttering "thanks" as he rolls over to rock himself back to sleep.

CHAPTER XVI

Birthday
December 8, 1941
Day: Four Hundred and Forty

Clip-clop, clip-clop, clip-clop. Hearing the gurney, Paddy's heart sinks. It never comes anymore. He pushes the *chariot* to the door, peeks out; *Johnny cant, he's coming—things piled high on the gurney.*

"I see ya," Johnny Cant calls out.

"What's all that?" Paddy asks, as the gurney wheels by me into the room.

"A desk, a chair. Can't ya see?"

"That's why you brought the gurney?"

"Why else? Ain't gonna lug this stuff on my back, am I?"

"You're not taking me somewhere?"

"Nope."

Relieved, Paddy follows him into the room while trying to get a good look at the desk and chair.

"They're for me, right?"

"Yup—a present. Ya birthday, ain't it?"

"Yeah, I'm six now. Got a box of fancy chocolates from Nurse Kelly. All kinds. We ate some already. Want one?"

"Don't eat candy. Where ya want it?" Johnny Cant lifts the desk from the gurney.

"In front of the window. Okay?"

"Fine with me."

As he places the desk before the window, Paddy quietly asks, not wanting to hurt his feelings, "Did you borrow it?"

Johnny Cant doesn't answer, just looks at Paddy, shaking his head, as if he had said something dumb.

"Hope you didn't. Nurse Edelstein will take it back for sure. She'll tell on you, too."

"She won't." He takes the chair from the gurney and sets it front of the desk. "Here, try it on for size."

Paddy pushes himself up from the *chariot,* walks to the desk, and slides into the seat.

"Boy, it's keen." He smiles, sitting up straight.

"Take a peek inside. The top opens," Johnny Cant says over his shoulder while heading the gurney toward the door. "And Happy Birthday."

"See you. Thanks." Paddy waves without looking as he runs his fingers over the glossy wood top of his new desk, which slants up to a flat place with a slot in it. Stretching over to his nightstand, he gets his Crayola box, removes a red, a blue, and a green crayon, and places them in the slot. Lifting the desk top, he looks look inside. A new comic book; the *man of steel* is on the cover looking fierce—legs astride, hands on his hips, an eagle on his shoulder—ready for action.

Paddy lowers the top, leaving the comic for later, folds his hands on the desk, and looks out the window. Large flakes of snow are drifting down: *Looks like feathers.*

Then, suddenly, he hears the wonderful voice coming from behind him, "Hay, lad!"

He spins around, almost toppling from the desk chair.

"Pop! Mom!" he shouts out. "What—what are you doing here?"

"Sure, to visit you, what else," his mom answers with a big smile as she enters the room behind his pop.

Paddy pushes up from the desk chair, awkwardly swinging the long brace out from under it. Happy tears swelling his eyes.

"Stay put, son—stay put!" his pop says, motioning for him to sit down. Turning to the door, he calls out, "Okay, come in. Come in!"

A girl walks into the room carrying a package in each hand. Gazing at her for a moment, Paddy looks to his mom.

"Who's that?" he asks softly as his mom comes up beside him.

She laughs quietly, "Sure, 'tis your sister, your sister Kate."

"Hi, Paddy. Happy birthday!" Kate calls out, all smiles.

"Wow! Gee—it's you. You're big now!"

"Was nine in March." Kate walks over and places the packages beside him on the desk.

"A proper young lady!" says Pop proudly while his mom bends over and kisses his cheek, whispering, "You look gran' darlin'."

Paddy can't keep his eyes off Kate. thinking: She's so—so different. Not like before, not at all.

Kate puts her coat on the empty bed, plops beside it looking around the room while Pop takes his mom's coat and slides a chair up beside the desk for her. She sits down placing a cane on alongside the packages.

"Where did you get the bike?" Kate calls over to him.

"From Ma Gillick."

"Who's that?"

"She does my physiotherapy."

"Physiotherapy?"

"She helps me with exercises and stuff."

"Oh, it's a nice bike."

"Open your presents," Mom says, as Pop places their coats on the empty bed beside Kate.

"Yeah!" He takes the smaller of the two packages from the desk.

"It's a clay modeling set. I wrapped it," Kate says, bouncing from the bed as he tears the blue paper from under a thick red ribbon.

"That's great." Paddy gazes at the box unsure of what's inside.

"It's a clay modeling set," Kate comes up next to him.

"Oh," he smiles up at her and then attacks the second package; a long box wrapped in brown paper and tied with string. Yanking away the string, he pulls the paper from a long box.

"From Mr. Harmon," Pop says. "You remember. lives upstairs in 403. Does the Red Ryder for the funny pages. Asked me to give it to you as we

On the box is a picture of Red Ryder, standing tall with a rifle over his shoulder. Behind him, Thunder's long brown and white face gazes friendly-like over the cowboy's shoulder.

"It opens at the end," Pop says. "'Here, I'll 'elp' you."

"No, I got it, Pop." He pulls opens the end of the box, reaches inside, and lifts out Mr. Harmon's gift.

"Holy cow—this is great!" He smiles.

"It's a genuine *Red Ryder Popgun*—see, 'is signature's on the stock," Pop says. "Let's show you how it works."

"Yes," Paddy hands the rifle over.

"First, you pump the lever, 'ere under the trigger." His pop shifts the lever up and down three times. "And you put the cork into the gun barrel—like so."

Then, aiming at the wall, he pulls the trigger, sending the cork flying from the gun, only to be stopped abruptly in midair.

"If it wasn't for the tether attaching the cork to the gun barrel," Pop laughs, "it would have gone through the bricks into the 'allway. 'Ere, give it a go."

Paddy takes the rifle, struggles to pump the stiff lever, loads the cork, and turns the gun on Kate. She backs away, and he fires.

"You missed," she laughs, jumping aside.

"Paddy—you don't want to be shootin' that 'ting' at your sister," his mom says sharply.

"Your mum's right, son," Pop warns. "The cork could pull free—you must be careful. Don't be point'n it at anyone. Understand?"

"Yes." Paddy nods, admiring Red Ryder's signature which looks to be burnt into the wooden stock by a branding iron.

"Now, put rifle aside," his pop says. "Walk a bit. Show us how you're get'n on."

"Sure, Pop."

Placing the popgun on his desk, Paddy stands, steadies himself, and slowly walks around the room, stepping forward strongly with the right leg and short brace while trying not to bend sideways as he swings the left leg long brace forward.

"Good, lad—very good."

"Thanks." He smiles, his legs shaking from the excitement more than the effort.

"How about riding the bike?" says Kate eagerly.

"Aye!" Pop agrees. "Let's see you do that."

"Sure, Bill, let the child rest a moment," his mom mildly objects.

"It's okay, Mom," Paddy says gladly, looking forward to showing off. "Let's go!" Kate jumps from bed.

"Down the hallway," Paddy says smiling brightly at his sister.

He makes his way to the tricycle, climbs on, places his feeble left foot under the pedal strap provided by Mr. Lombardi, and off they go—Kate leading the way.

"Race ya," she says when they are outside the door.

"'Alf-a-mo," Pop calls from the room, "your mam wants to watch."

With their parents standing in the doorway, they head down the hallway, Paddy leaning over the handlebars going all out while Kate skips alongside him—both happily laughing.

As Paddy reaches the far end of the hallway, going faster than ever, he turns the handlebars sharply to swing around. The tricycle tips up, and over it goes—bike, braces, and Paddy smashing to the floor.

"God!" Kate screams, stopping dead in her tracks.

Sprawled on his side, smiling weakly, he looks up at her and mutters, "I'm okay. I'm okay."

"He all right, Kate!" Mom calls out.

"I'm okay," Paddy hollers back, trying to free his feeble foot from the pedal strap.

"He's not hurt," Kate shouts, leaning over to help her brother get up.

"Kate, leave 'im be!" their pop says, walking briskly to them.

"I'll help him, Pop," she insists.

"No! Leave 'im," he repeats firmly. "'E's got to do it on 'is own."

"I can get up—no trouble." Paddy motions Kate away.

As Pop and Kate watch, he untangles himself from the tricycle and works his way to his feet, as Ma Gillick taught him, trying not to look klutzy. Standing, trembling a little, he rights the tricycle, mounts-up, and returns the feeble left foot to its place under the strap.

"Race ya back!" He grins embarrassingly at Kate.

She looks to her father. He nods, yes.

And they take off again back down the hallway—their pop jogging behind, their mom in the doorway groaning, "Oh, Lard!"

"You did good, lad," Pop says, ruffling Paddy's hair when they're all back in the room.

"Indeed," Mom chimes in, "but you must be careful."

Then, taking his coat from the empty bed, Pop says, "Back in a bit."

"Where you goin'?" Paddy asks.

"To the car to listen to President Roosevelt. 'E's on the radio at two o'clock," he answers over his shoulder.

"Why? Why do you want to do that?"

His pop stops and turns to his son. "Ah, you don't know, do you? The Japs—they attacked Pearl 'Arbor yesterday."

"Japs?"

"The Japanese," Kate says jumping back on the empty bed while Pop strolls from the room, "they dropped hundreds of bombs on Pearl Harbor."

Paddy pedals over to her.

"That's an island in the Pacific Ocean some place. It's all they talk about on the radio—none of the good shows were even on last night."

* * *

When Pop leaves, Paddy and Kate then shoot the Red Ryder pop gun for a while. After that, they sit on the empty bed and make houses and people with the clay from the modeling set. And with Mom resting in her chair, Paddy gets all the news:

Mom: "Yer cousins Patsy an' Betty as you know are in St. Joseph's Home."

Paddy: "They like it?"

Mom: "Sure, 'tis a lovely place with the saintly Franciscan Nuns bein' so good an' kind—God love 'em."

Kate: "I really miss them, though, and Forrest Hills, too. Albany, it's not that nice. The house is cold. The back yard is full of junk. And there're rats, too—big as cats."

Paddy: "I don't like rats. We got squirrels but they're nice."

Mom: "It'll be all cleaned up. An' your dad is fixin' a place in the back yard for a vegetable garden—it'll be fine."

Kate: "He's killing the rats, too. Blood and guts get all over the big traps—yuck!"

Mom: "Mrs. Beck, who lives upstairs and owns the house, is mindin' little Billy today."

Kate: "She's real fat and she smells bad."

Mom: "It's her cancer, Kate. You must be charitable towards the paur soul."

Kate: "And she's not nice, mostly."

Mom: "Little Billy is nine months old now. He walks some, holdin' on. Hardly ever cries—a good child."

Kate: "But can he screech. I mean loud—hurt your ears. Wait 'till you hear him. And boy, does he have stinky diapers—I mean, very stinky. Then getting changed, he pees up in the air like a fountain."

Mom: "Sure, we all get a good laugh at that."

Kate: "Billy's so cute like, though. He wants to play all the time. You'll have loads fun with him when you get home."

Paddy: "Mom, when can I go home? When will that be? I want to see him."

Mom: "Won't be long now, God willing—now what have you been up ter?"

Paddy tells them all about going to the clinic and his exercises, his visits to Miss Minnie—but not her and Johnny Cant hugging and kissing, Nurse Edelstein's lessons, swimming and prayers with Mr. Cooney; he shows them the holy cards, which his mom really likes. And while he is reciting the *Apostles' Creed* for them, as his mom requested, Pop comes marching back into the room.

"Nan, President Roosevelt 'as declared war on Japan!" He throws his coat on the empty bed. "I'm join'n up."

"Your what?" She turns to him, pulling herself up in her chair.

"I'm join'n up."

"What's that mean?"

"Go'n in the Navy, Nan."

She laughs. "Sure, they'd be hard-up to take an auld goat like yerself."

"It's war! They need experienced seamen. That's me, ten years at sea under me belt—I'm go'n!"

"Yer'ill do no such thing, Bill!" she says, her voice quivering.

He walks over to inspect the *Britannia* sitting proudly on the nightstand beside his wife.

Making a sniffing sound and crunching her face, she growls looking up at him, "You've been drinkin', yer 'ave!"

"Pop," Paddy speaks up loudly, not wanting them quarreling, "Mr. Cooney, he's going to let me sail it—her—in the pool!"

"'E is, is 'e?" his pop lifts one of the *Britannia's* hatch covers and looks idly inside the hull.

"Yes—and soon."

"I'll be sail'n meself soon." He replaces the hatch cover.

"You really going, Pop?" Kate asks.

"He's half-stewed, Kate. 'Tis the drink talkin'—he's goin' nowhere," her mom responds angrily.

"Nan, it's war. We'll soon be take'n on Germany as well. I'll do me part!"

"'Tis us you want to be lookin' after. That's your part, Bill," she answers, her voice now calm.

Turning from the *Britannia*, he grabs his coat from the bed and walks toward the door.

"Where you think your goin' now?"

"To listen for more news," he says, without looking back.

"The the whiskey your goin' for!" she yells after him. "An' go ahead—join up! Good-riddance-ter-bad-rubbish!"

* * *

Inside *Lilburn House,* a white mansion with a lofty four columned portico, the receptionist takes their coats and leads them into a high-ceilinged room containing a scattering of turn-of-the-century furniture. And they settle into leather wing-backed chairs, Nan and Kate together on one side of a large Oriental rug, Bill across from them.

Bill, eying the décor after the receptionist leaves, calls to Nan. "It's like Windsor Castle."

"Be expectin' the Queen any moment," she calls back with a chuckle. "Think I'm dressed fittingly?"

"Oh, aye, Nan—ya the cat's meow."

As they both laugh noisily, Kate, sitting straight-up lady-like, whispers to her, "Shush, Mom. You and Pop are talking too loud."

"Shush, yerself!" She turns to her snappily. "'Tis not a church we're at."

Bill rises from his chair and saunters to the center of the Oriental rug. Looking up, he circles under a large crystal chandelier, as if inspecting its safety. He then continues on to a large etching hanging between two tall windows. He stops before it, leans forward, hands clasped behind his back: four men in nineteenth century hunting dress sitting around a table drinking from tall goblets, a collie dog curled at their feet.

"Ah, a comfortable lot," he sighs softly.

Stepping to the window left of the picture, he looks out. "Nan," he says loudly, "you could see the Hudson River from 'ere if it weren't for the snow—really come'n down now."

"Hadn't we better be leavin' soon?" she shouts back.

"Aye, sooner the better."

Kate shifts in her chair, wanting to *shush* them again when the receptionist appears in the doorway.

"Will you please follow me?" she says softly.

Kate jumps to her feet while Bill walks quickly over to assist Nan up from her chair.

"Stay where ya at, Kate," he quietly orders.

With a pout, she plops back into her chair.

* * *

"Please come in. Have a seat." Dr. Strasburg glances up from behind a massive desk as Bill and Nan enter the spacious office. "Have a seat."

He gestures toward the two chairs in front of his desk and returns his attention to the folder opened before him.

"'Tis posh...an' all them shelves of books, Bill," Nan whispers as she sinks into the soft leather, placing her cane across her lap.

"Aye, impressive," Bill says softly, taking his seat.

After watching the doctor flip through a folder for a few moments, Bill speaks up, "Nice old place you got 'ere, Dr. Strasburg."

"Yes, yes," he mumbles, raising his eyes as if seeing them for the first time. "Dates back to the late 1700's. Part of the *Lilburn Estate* purchased by the *State Legislature* in 1905."

"Lovely place." Nan smiles.

"Indeed." Dr. Strasburg sits back in his chair. "It is a refined Georgian design in the Palladian style, mostly original furnishing and all that—but on days like this, it's somewhat drafty. So, then, you had a good visit with Paddy?"

"O' aye," Bill says. "Walked for us. Rode 'is bicycle. 'E was in high spirits when. Particularly glad to see his sister."

Addressing Nan, Dr. Strasburg asks, "And how have you been?"

"Her nerves been act'n up lately," Bill answers, assuming the doctor is inquiring about her multiple sclerosis. "Sound as a pound she was all summer. The last few months though, her legs been give'n out lately. Been quick-tempered as well, argue'n at the drop of a 'at, and..."

"Ach! For God's sake, Bill!" Nan pokes his thigh with her cane. "Cut yer bellachin'. We're here about Paddy. Let's get on with it, lest we be snowed in."

Dr. Strasburg looks curiously at them for a moment and then drops his eyes back to the folder.

"First a trifle matter." He lifts a sheet of paper from the folder. "This note from Nurse Edelstein saying Paddy often 'head rocks' himself to sleep at night."

"Head rocks?" Nan looks uncertainly from the doctor to Bill.

"In Paddy's case, Nurse Edelstein says, 'he rhythmically rocks his forehead into his pillow'. It is not uncommon," Dr. Strasburg returns the note to the folder, "for children confined to hospitals and orphanages to sooth themselves this way during difficult and lonely times; a self-comforting ritual that helps them fall asleep."

Bill and Nan stare at the doctor for a moment, dumbfounded.

"God love 'em," Nan sighs, dabbing a tear from her cheek.

"What's to done about it?" Bill asks.

"Nothing to do. Just information for you. In mentally normal children, the behavior usually goes away as a usual part of development, although it can continue throughout life. Well now, to more serious matters." Dr. Strasburg consults his folder. "Let's see, Paddy has been with us about a year."

"Been fourteen months, now," Nan corrects him, shaking the "head rocking" from her mind.

"Aye—fourteen months," Bill agrees.

Looking up, Dr. Strasburg smiles.

"Yes, admitted October 11, 1940. Today is December 8, 1941. About fourteen months."

Turning papers in the folder, he goes on.

"On October 12, the day after he was admitted, both his legs were immobilized in a full plaster-of-Paris cast for, let's see, for two months and..."

"Oh, no! That's not correct," Nan interrupts. "Paddy had them awful casts with the bar between 'em for almost three months. Am I not right, Bill?"

"Aye, as ever." He nods.

Dr. Strasburg looks at Nan. "Yes, I'll be more precise. On January 10, 1941, the casts were removed—that's three months."

She nods in agreement.

"Then on January 24, 1941," he continues, "Paddy began physiotherapy. March 3rd, two months later, he started wearing full-braces on both legs and a few weeks later his right brace was shortened to a half-brace—below the knee." Looking again at Nan, he says, "Does that all seem correct?"

"Yes, I think so."

"So," Dr. Strasburg closes the folder, "the question now is where we go from here?" Opening a small gold case on his desk, he removes a cigarette, and slides the case toward Bill and Nan. "Smoke if you like."

Bill stands, takes a cigarette, and places it behind his ear, nodding thank you. Nan declines with a wave of her hand.

Dr. Strasburg lights up and tilts back in his chair. "After ten months of physiotherapy, your boy's right leg has responded well. However, his left leg is still very weak. Although both legs are quite atrophied, the left is more so. And the left foot, it is essentially non-responsive. Also..."

"Ask about the Sister Kenny," Nan murmurs, probing Bill gently with her cane.

"Aye, Dr. Strasburg," Bill cuts the doctor short, "we saw this story in *Life Magazine* about Sister Kenny. A picture of her, too, in this big hat—look'n like Admiral Nelson himself."

"She's not at all like that sorry scoundrel," Nan says with a sharp look at Bill. "She's a handsome woman, she is."

Then, turning to Dr. Strasburg, she says, "Sister Kenny said usin' casts—as you did with Paddy—stops the muscles from developin' makin' 'em worst."

"Nan," Bill says, "leave it be. We want to move on."

"Well," Dr. Strasburg rocks forward, tapping cigarette ash into a glass ashtray, "I'm quite familiar with *Sister Kenny* and her crusade against immobilization. However, the woman is misguided. She does not understand that the procedure is necessary, especially for children whose soft bones are growing and easily deformed by the muscle imbalances caused by polio."

"She's had great success usin' hot packs, she has. An' her exercises..." Nan continues.

"Success," Dr. Strasburg stumps his cigarette out in the ashtray, his voice rising as his words rush out, "that's highly questionable. *Her* claims that *her* treatments prevent deformities and speeds recovery have been roundly debunked by the medical profession—even by her own *Australian Medical Association*. This so-called *sister* Kenny is a tireless self-promoter. And claiming to be a trained nurse. She's not. She says she has a college degree—she has no such degree..."

"Sure," Nan breaks in angrily, "Paddy's gettin' exercise, is he not? That's what Sister Kenny does, too, but no casts?"

"Nan, calm down," Bill says, patting her arm.

She pulls her arm away and sits quietly.

"Yes, of course," Dr. Strasburg goes on, sitting back in his chair, voice now taking on a calm, professional tone, "after the acute stage, when immobilization is no longer *required*, we use a variety of modalities in our physiotherapy—short wave diathermy, ultraviolet lamps, whirlpool, as well as exercise, massage, and manipulation. Our goals are essentially twofold. First, strengthen the muscle fibers not destroyed by the disease. Second, to reeducate these healthy fibers to take over at least some of functioning lost with the paralyzed fibers.

"We are not trying to revive damaged motor neurons, as Ms. Kenny suggests she does." His voice rises slightly. "That is not possible. Polio is not a muscle disease, as she believes. It is a disease of the central nervous system. Do you understand?"

Nan slumps in her chair. "Yes—it seems we *must* understand—but is there more to be done now for the child."

"Continue his physiotherapy to strengthen whatever muscle fibers remains viable." Dr. Strasburg grins at her as if he had won a small battle. "Train him to walk as best he can. Work to get full extension of the left leg, which still does not straighten as it should. In addition, we could improve the function and stability of his left foot. It is almost useless now."

"Aye, you can fix the foot?" Bill asks shifting forward in his chair.

"Yes, somewhat. It would require an operation."

"Lard-save-us. We'll have none of that—no operation!" Nan responds abruptly.

"Just a moment, Nan," Bill says calmly. "What would you do, doctor?"

"We would rearrange tendons in his foot and fuse his big toe. This procedure would stabilize his foot and ultimately improve his gait, his walking."

"Ay don't know, doctor." Bill shakes his head. "He's get'n along fine as 'e is."

"Yes, that's true. He is *getting along*, but his mobility will remain limited by the flaccid foot, together with the atrophy, unless we take corrective measures. And it is likely, highly likely, he will always have to rely on a brace, at least on his left leg."

"Corrective measures—an operation?" Nan sighs, looking at Bill.

"Yes, but that, of course, is up to you." Dr. Strasburg takes another cigarette from the gold box.

Sitting back in his chair, he lights-up, lifts his chin, and puffs out a perfect circle of smoke. Bill and Nan watch as it floats up from his puckered lips, twisting lazily into a figure eight.

* * *

"He knows 'is stuff, Nan," Bill argues as they return unescorted to the anteroom. "We must listen. He's a doctor—a smart man."

"Smart, smarter than a dumber one, I'm sure," Nan answers.

Kate springs to her feet, rushing to them as they enter the room. "What happened?"

"Noth'n," Bill answers sharply. "Help ya mum to the car. I'll run ahead, warm it up."

"Bill," Nan says tiredly, "no drink now. You have to drive in all that snow."

"I'm just go'n to warm-up the car," Bill replies impatiently and rushes off.

The snow has stopped and the gray sky is fading into night as mother and daughter negotiate the steps down from the *Lilburn House* portico.

"What did the doctor say, mom?" Kate asks. "How is Paddy?"

"He's no worse than he has to be," she replies, probing the next icy step with her cane while contemplating the long, snowy trudge to the parking lot.

Walking in silence, Kate holding her mom's arm, they finally reach the car. Kate opens the rear door to be greeted by warmth, the faint smell of whiskey, and the familiar baritone voice of John W. Vandercoock reporting the latest news:

> *A declaration of war with Japan has been approved by the House and Senate, with one dissenting vote, as Congress demands to know what happened at Pearl Harbor and why we were taken by surprise...*

Pushing the passenger seat forward, she climbs into the back of the car. Her mom returns the seat and clumsily works her way into it. Handing her cane back to Kate, she pulls the door shut.

"Turn that off, Bill," she demands. "We'll be hearin' enough of it."

Click: the radio goes silent.

The snow has been cleared, and there is little traffic as they drive north on route 9W toward Albany. Kate, stretched out on the back seat, is quickly asleep. Nan soon dozes off as well.

Glancing at his wife, her head rocking with the rhythm of the car, Bill leans forward, fishes under the seat, and retrieves a pint of Four Roses. He unscrews the cap, takes a long swig, and with a satisfying sigh recaps the bottle returning it to its hideaway. Recharged, he turns the radio on low:

> *A blackout took effect 20 minutes ago all across the West Coast. It's not working too well yet. In San Diego, the FBI, with the cooperation*

of the Mexican government, tonight checked unconfirmed reports of armed bands of Japanese in lower California. Fifty unidentified planes have been sighted flying from the southwest toward San Francisco...

Four miles outside of Newburgh, it begins snowing again. Easing the Chevy through a long curve, Bill reaches forward and switches on the window wipers. As the wipers spring into action, the headlights catch patch of ice. He grips the steering wheel tightly, taps the brakes. The back-end slides toward the median. Neck tense, arms rigid, frightened, he taps again, pulling the steering wheel. The *ol' jalopy* whirls full-circle across the oncoming traffic lane, rumbles headlong down a twenty-foot embankment, and crashes, downing a tall pine.

* * *

In the curtained cubical, a young doctor leans over Nan stitching an inch-long gash above her swollen left eye— the cheek below a puffed angry purple.

Bill, chest bruised by the steering wheel, and Kate, distraught but uninjured, wait patiently in the deserted lobby. It has been two hours since the ambulance brought them to Newburgh Hospital. A tired looking nurse finally approaches and leads father and daughter down a long, dreary corridor.

"How you do'n, Nan?" Bill asks softly, entering the cubicle ahead of Kate. "See they got you all patched up."

With a twisted smile, Nan wheezes, "I'll be fine after I lie here a bit. But you must call an' check on the baby. Tell Mrs. Beck what's happened an' when we'll be home."

"O' aye, I'll take care of it."

"Can I do something, Mom?" Kate leans over and kisses her mother's bandaged forehead.

"Thank you, darlin', but no. I'm fine." She caresses Kate's cheek.

"Noth'n you can do right now, Kate," her pop adds, turning to leave. "Just stay with ya mum. I'll be back in a while."

Over the next hour, Bill arranges for the disposal of the car, which is totaled. He checks on the next bus to *Albany,* not until 7:45 A.M. Lastly, he phones Mrs. Beck. Little Billy is fast asleep.

Nan is sleeping when he returns to the cubicle. Kate, slouched a chair, is flipping through a *Look Magazine.*

"How ya mam?" he asks quietly.

"Okay. She's been asleep all the time." Kate looks groggily up at him. "When can we go home?"

"Come-on." He motions with his head for her to follow him.

Taking seats in the lobby, Bill explains about the car and that they must take a bus to Albany but can't get one until the morning.

"We'll be here all night?" She sobs softly, a stream of tears suddenly flowing down her cheek.

"Aye, afraid so." Bill slides his arm over Kate's shoulder, gently pulling her close. "Ya mam, she'll be fine. And we'll be home before you know it."

* * *

Sometime during the night, the doctor who stitched Nan's wound shakes Bill shoulder.

"Aye?" he opens his eyes.

"Please, come with me," the doctor says wearily.

Following the doctor, Bill glances across the lobby at Kate coiled in her coat sleeping on a couch. They proceed down the corridor toward the cubicle. When they get to it, the doctor continues. Bill's heart sinks. The curtain is pulled back. The table is empty. A few yards farther along, they enter a small office.

"Please, have a seat," the doctor says, collapsing into a chair behind a small steel desk.

"Someth'n happen to Nan?" Bill sits down in a wooden chair beside the desk.

Looking at him for a moment, the doctor says, "Your wife has had a miscarriage."

"What!" Bill jerks back, about tipping his chair over. "She was pregnant?"

"Yes, about two or three months along, I'd say."

"I'll be damned—how's she, now?" He shakes his head searching his jacket for his cigarettes.

"She's fine. We've moved her to a room upstairs. I gave her something to help her sleep. She should be able to leave in the morning."

"There's a bus to Albany at 7:45." Bill extends a pack of cigarettes toward the doctor. "Pregnant—Christ—can't believe it."

The doctor accepts the offer with a nod.

CHAPTER XVII

Joey
December 12, 1941
Day: Four Hundred and Forty-eight

Paddy rolls to a dead stop. The bed curtain is pulled around the empty bed. He pedals into the room—stops again. Nurse Kelly is talking quietly behind the curtain. He tries to listen, can't make out what she's saying. Continuing over to his desk, he climbs from the tricycle and slides into his desk chair, being careful not to bash the braces against the desk. Slowly, quietly, he lifts the desktop and removes a *Superman* comic. Paging through it, he waits.

After what seems like forever, he hears the curtain slide open and close on the far side of the bed. Nurse Kelly appears, smiles at him, and walks over.

"How was the clinic?" she asks softly, squatting beside the desk.

"Good," he answers, looking beyond her at the closed curtain. "Someone in the empty bed?"

She puts her finger to her lips. "Talk softly—you got yerself a roommate."

"A roommate? Wow!"

"Sh-sh—he's sleepin'. Speak softly." She puts her finger to her lips.

"What's his name?" he whispers.

"Joey."

"How old is he?"

"Two years older than you—eight, almost nine."

"Will he be here like my roommate for good?"

"Yes, for some time. Now stay quiet. Let 'im rest. Be back later."

"Okay."

He smiles as she stands, playfully pinching his nose.

After Nurse Kelly tiptoes from the room, Paddy glances again at the *Superman* comic, but he's so jittery that he can hardly make out the pictures.

"Hay, can you come here?" A sickly voice, low and horse, comes from behind the curtain.

"You mean now?" he answers nervously.

"What ya think, next week? Yeah, now."

Tossing the comic on his bed, Paddy rises from the desk chair and shuffles over to the far side of the once empty bed and ease back the curtain.

"Hi," Joey says.

He's curled on his side, a wide bandage around his head, and looking at Paddy. His eyes are large, brown, sunken in dark hollows.

"Hi, my name's Paddy."

"Yeah, the nurse told me. What's wrong with you?"

"Polio, in my legs."

"Oh, I know about that. Rocco, he's my stupid cousin, he got it. He's in an iron lung."

"I was in that for a while when I was four. Don't remember much about it."

"How old are you now."

"Just six last week."

Rolling over on his back, Joey struggles into a sitting position. His body seems small while his head looks extra big and scrunches down between his shoulders.

He has no neck, Paddy thinks to himself.

"Rocco's gonna die. Aunt Rosie told my mom that. I heard it." He scoots himself back against two pillows propped up at the top of the bed.

"Wow, when?"

"She didn't say. Soon."

"What about you? What do you have?" Paddy asks.

"Spina bifida."

"What's that?"

"My spinal cord sticks out from my back. Happened before I was born."

"Oh. Then why's your head all bandaged up then?"

"Got water on the brain, too." He grins, as if he has said something funny.

"Water—on the brain?"

"Yeah, builds up inside my head. Got a tube from there to my stomach. It empties out the water so my skull don't burst or brain get smooched." He grins again. "They opened my head at Brooklyn Hospital last week to make the tube longer because I've grown."

"Does it hurt—the tube?"

"Nah, only when I laugh." Another grin.

"How come only when you laugh?"

"Only when I laugh! That's a joke."

"Oh." Paddy smiles, a little embarrassed.

"How long you been here?" Joey asks.

"A long time—since way before Christmas. But I'm going home soon. Just have to a walk better."

"I can't walk. My legs, they don't move much. Here, wanna see?"

With a sweep of his hand, Joey throws his covers aside. Paddy, startled, jerks away from the bed, grabbing the mattress to keep from tumbling backwards. Steadying himself, he stares at Joey's legs. They're short, stubby-like, and his feet are twisted inward as if broken.

"What happened to your feet?"

"Born that way, too—called *clubfoot*. They look like clubs," Joey pulls his teeth over his lower lip into an oddly funny face. "Don't they?"

"I guess—you don't mind showing them?"

"No big deal. Everyone wants to look—should charge 'em. Make a bundle." He laughs quietly and then leans over the side of the bed. "Now, let's see your polio legs."

"No." Paddy shakes his head.

"Showed you mine. So show me yours."

"I don't like people looking. Anyway, I got the braces on and pants."

"Take 'em off."

"No." He shakes his head again.

"Okay." Joey pushes himself upright. "Show ya my back? Sticks out like a balloon."

"No, not now."

"Don't blame you." He covers himself. "Ya like it here?"

"It's okay," Paddy answers, relieved the stubby legs and clubfeet are gone.

"At Brooklyn Hospital everyone was mostly mean—like the Negro guy who brought me to the room here."

"In a gurney—with a broke wheel?"

"Yeah."

"He's not mean—not at all." Paddy laughs. "That's Johnny Cant. He just seems that way sometimes, like Nurse Edelstein. She seems mean, too, at first."

"Who's nurse...?"

"Nurse Edelstein, that's the night nurse. She's teaching me to read and do arithmetic. And boy she's strict, not like Nurse Kelly."

"Nurse Kelly—the one that just left?"

"Yes. She's always nice, mostly. Funny, too."

"Who else you know here?"

"Well, there's Ma Gillick. She does my physiotherapy. She's pretty, like a movie star. And Mr. Cooney, he's teaching me to swim good. Mr. Martin brings the food tray—he's funny and limps. And Miss Minnie in the kitchen..."

"Stop!" Joey shouts in his croaky voice. "I mean—like kids! You know—other kids."

"No, not really."

"What. Ya don't know any. Or there ain't none?"

"There's lots. Saw them at the Christmas party—all big kids. They stay in wards and go to school. But I don't see them all the time, just sometimes in the hallways."

"Oh," Joey says, frowning.

"Want to see some of my comics? Mostly *Superman*," Paddy asks. "I get them from Johnny Cant. And sometimes my Pop brings *Red Ryder* ones."

"Sure," Joey says brightly. "Superman—he's great."

Paddy turns away, nearly stumbling over myself as he rushes to get comics for Joey—my roommate!

CHAPTER XVIII

Second Christmas Party
December 19, 1941
Day: Four Hundred and Fifty-five

Joey's voice is much better. And he talks all the time, entertaining Paddy to no end. "Yer full ter the ears with words," she teased him once as he waxed away. Joey contemplated that idea for a second. Then grinning at her, he said in his contrived Brooklyn, tough guy tone—which he often uses around Paddy and Johnny Cant, Nurse Kelly sometimes, too, but never Nurse Edelstein who would be forever correcting him—"Ya know Nurse Kellywithout this here," he stroked the bandage wrapped around his head, "the words would all just burst through my skull like from a can of Campbell's alphabet soup." She laughed hard at that.

Joey's favorite topic is baseball.

"The Brooklyn Dodgers, they're the best team," he says. "And Pee Wee Reese, he plays shortstop—that's the hardest position right between 2nd and 3rd base—he's the best player." Joey has assured Paddy, that he knows everything about the game—"everything." His dad and brother Tony even took him to Ebbets Field, he told him proudly. "That's the home of the Dodgers. We sat in a box. They're the real best seats. And Mayor LaGuardia, he was in the box right next to us. He shook my hand, Papa and Tony's, too, and said we could come visit him at Gracie Mansion. That's where New York mayors live. And we're going to go, for sure."

Comic books are Joey next favorite thing. He reads them over and over again. Sometimes he reads them to Paddy, making different voices for Clark Kent and for Superman—Lois Lane, too. And in the evening, after Paddy finishes his lessons, Nurse Edelstein lets Joey read aloud from *Treasure Island,* that she is reading to them. But he doesn't make voices, not even for Long John Silver which Paddy would like, guessing, probably correctly, that Nurse Edelstein wouldn't put up with that.

Also, Joey has a radio. It came the day after he arrived. It was from Tony, who is in the army now. On the package was printed, DO NOT OPEN UNTIL CHRISTMAS. But Joey ripped right into it.

The radio looks "real keen," as Joey said. Its dark wood, shaped like church window, and has an eye above the tuning dial that lights up when the set is turned on. Listening is *restricted,* however. Nurse Kelly puts on music sometimes during the day, and they are allowed to hear the five o'clock stories—*The Lone Ranger, Sky King,* and best of all, *Superman.* When *Superman* comes on, they love to repeat, loudly, along with the announcer:

Faster than an airplane!
More powerful than a locomotive!
Impervious to bullets!
Up in the sky-look!
It's a giant bird!
It's a plane!
It's Superman!

Joey says Nurse Kelly will let them listen to the Dodger games when the baseball season starts. He is "workin' on that."

When not reading comics or listening to the five o'clock stories, or talking baseball, Joey loves to entertain Paddy with stories about Brooklyn and his papa's barbershop. It's called *Angelo's,* after his papa. Actually, *Angelo's* is a bit more than a barbershop, according to Joey. Only his Uncle Louie cuts the hair and gives the shaves.

"Papa and Uncle Ralph," Joey explained, "they stay in a room in the back of the shop where people go to borrow money. It's a barber shop but like a bank, too. And when guys don't pay the money back, Uncle Ralph goes and talks to them."

Joey, his dad, mom, sisters Nina and Marcella, brother Tony, and grandma Nonna all live together in an apartment above the barbershop. It's a great place, Joey said. He and Tony share a bedroom. "That's where Tony tells me things. Like all about girls," Joey told Paddy confidentially. "Tony, he really knows about lots, a really good stuff."

And on nice summer days, Joey's mom fixes pillows on the back fire escape so he can watch the "old guys" playing bocce ball down in the yard. What they do, as Joey described the game, is roll balls, like baseballs but wood, to see who gets closest to a littler ball. "It's dumb," Joey said, "but they talk baseball, in Italian, and that's real fun to listen to." Joey claims to speak Italian "some."

Also, Joey and grandma Nonna watch the "big kids" from the front window playing stickball in the street. "Nonna sits at the window all day looking out to see what's happening. She never watches out the back," Joey explained. "She thinks old guys are *stupido*—that means stupid."

Stickball is like baseball, "but different," Joey said describing the game. "You hit a pink, high bouncing, rubber ball, called a *Spaldeen*, with a broomstick bat. In most games, the hitter throws the ball up and bats it on the fly or after a bounce. That's *fungo* stickball. But for big important games, there's always a pitcher, and the ball is hit on one bounce. And a good pitcher, he puts English on the ball to make it jump right, or left, when it bounces, or skips fast at you. So, it's fuckin' hard to hit."

"Stickball players say fuckin' all the time," Joey said, introducing Paddy to the word. "Like, if a player strikes out, he'll yell—ah! fuck! If he hits a homerun—it's fuckin'-a! When a car is coming—everyone hollers fuckin' car! And when real mad at someone, they curse 'em out with—fuck you! Things like that."

When Paddy asked what fuckin' means, Joey laughed. "That's the word for getting babies—*stupido*."

Joey says fuckin' sometimes when it's just the two of them in the room, like, "The fucken' food here stinks." After Paddy tried saying it, Joey snickered, "Ya sound fag-ie—like a girl." So, he leaves the "f" word to Joey.

* * *

They are now waiting for Johnny Cant to take them to the Christmas Party. Paddy told Joey all about the last Christmas Party: the auditorium packed with kids, the pretty girl, the Santa kids singing, the reindeer story, the naughty boys and mean Nurse McCormick—he likes that part best—and getting candy at the end.

They have on Santa hats like those the Santa kids wore last Christmas. Nurse Kelly got the hats for them. Paddy is dressed as usual in shirt, pants, and braces. Joey has on Paddy's sailor suit, now too small for him. Joey wanted to wear the sailor hat, too, but it just perched on the top of his big, bandaged head like a nurse's hat.

Yesterday, in preparation for the holiday, Nurse Kelly helped them decorate the room. Paddy and Joey cut green and red paper and glued them together to make Christmas garlands, and she hung them all around.

Best of all, Nurse Kelly brought in her portable record player and a stack of records to play while they worked. And the *Irish Wash Women* started playing, to their great surprise and delight she stood at attention—arms stiff at her side, eyes focused straight ahead, face solemn. And she did an Irish Jig—her legs kicking and stomping the floor as if trampling an invading hoard of roaches. Joey and Paddy hooted and clapped like crazy.

Later, they each named the song they liked best. Paddy's was *Boogie Woogie Bugle Boy. Chattanooga Choo! Choo!* was Joey's. Nurse Kelly's favorite was *Green Eyes*—because she has green eyes, she said grinning as she lifted her eyebrows with her fingers to show them. It was great fun.

"What's that thing?" Joey says, smart-alecky like, as Johnny Cant finally arrives wheeling a different kind of gurney into the room.

It has low wooden sides, big wheelchair wheels in front, and small regular gurney wheels in back.

"Looks like a cart for selling vegetables like in my neighborhood."

"Yeah, a *vegetable cart*," Johnny Cant grumbles, pushing it up beside Joey's bed.

He lifts Joey into the *vegetable cart*, propping him up with pillows. He then puts Paddy in, and off they go to the Christmas party.

As they reach Times Square, Joey, who has been unusually silent, asks Johnny Cant, "You like baseball?"

"Yup."

"What's your favorite team?"

"Yankees—world champs."

"Mine's the Dodgers."

"Me, too," Paddy pipes up. "And Pee Wee Reese is our favorite player."

"*Pee Wee?* What's he, a midget or some'n'?" Johnny Cant laughs.

"He ain't no midget!" Joey responds. "He's almost six feet tall! And he's good, real good! We paid Boston $35,000 for him and four players. And last season, he was MVP, you know."

"But seems he ain't good 'nough," Johnny Cant comes back at him, softly.

"Ya can't say that—he's great!" Joey insists.

"Lost the World Series to my good ol' Yankees, didn't ya? An' what about Joe DiMaggio?"

Johnny Cant swings the *vegetable cart* down Broadway toward the auditorium entrance.

"Yeah, but..." Joey stops. With a great smile, he looks at Paddy.

They can hear faint talking and laughing coming down the hallway. Johnny Cant speeds up, the merriment getting louder and louder. A moment later they push through the large doors into the auditorium. The noise is ear shattering.

"See, Joey, like I told you—isn't it?" Paddy hollers above the racket while the *vegetable cart* moves up the aisle toward the balcony.

"Yeah! It's great!" Joey yells back, his eyes bouncing between the huge Christmas tree to all the kids.

While Johnny Cant maneuvers the *vegetable cart* into position under the balcony, Paddy searches the gurneys on either side of them and others around the room for the pretty girl. She's not there. He then hunts row by row for the naughty boys. No sign of them either. As he's about to inform Joey, he spots an empty seat near the front of the auditorium. There's just one. His heart jumps.

It's straight down the aisle in front of him, at the end of the row just behind were the Santa kids sit after singing. He smiles, thinking: *It's perfect—I know I can walk there! I'll be with the big kids. And Ma Gillick, she'll see me and wave when she comes out to play the piano.*

Johnny is standing close beside the *vegetable cart,* his back leaning against the wall. Paddy stretches over and tugs the sleeve of his white jacket.

"What?" Johnny Cant leans his toward him.

"I want to sit down there!" Paddy shouts above the noise, pointing toward the seat.

"Where?" He looks down the aisle.

"Down there! I want to go down there!" Paddy shouts again, pointing frantically toward the empty seat.

"Ya don't wanna stay here wi' ya buddy?"

"No! Hurry! Help me out! Someone will get it first!"

"Ya sure?"

"Yes, hurry—please!"

"Okay, okay. Hold ya horses."

"Where you going?" Joey calls out, as Johnny Cant lifts Paddy from the *vegetable wagon.*

"Down front. See you later," he yells back, not taking his eyes from the empty seat.

"Why?"

Ignoring Joey and holding the side of the *vegetable wagon* for support, Paddy looks down the aisle, the seat looking far away now.

"I'll help ya." Johnny Cant reaches for his hand.

"No." he pushes the hand away. "I can do it."

"Okay, suit-ya-self." Johnny Cant shrugs and moves back to his place against the wall.

Joey leans over the side of the *vegetable wagon*. "Hay, why...why ya leavin'?"

Paddy doesn't answer. He walks the four steps to the top of the aisle and stops, grabbing the back of the first seat. He looks toward the stage were the Santa kids are lining up. Legs shaking, he takes a deep breath and goes on. Swinging the long braced leg forward, he plants it and steps ahead with the half-braced leg. Feeling unsteady, legs shaking, he hurriedly grabs the next seatback before him. In this way, seatback-to-seatback, he slowly makes his way, trying hard to walk *normal*.

Halfway down the aisle, shaking head to toe now, he pauses looking up at the stage. The wheelchair Santa kids are lining up in front of the walk-ons. He then glances back up the aisle. Joey is watching him. He waves. Joey doesn't wave back. Looking away, he mumbles to himself, "He doesn't know how good I'm doing."

Paddy goes on. Finally, grasping the back of the empty seat, he takes a final step, turns, and falls heavily into it clanging the long brace against the seat in front.

On the stage, the Santa kids are all in place. The lights then dim. The auditorium gets quiet. Twisting around, Paddy smiles proudly up the aisle. Joey's eyes are still on him, but he turns quickly away. Paddy spins about mumbling again, "He's just jealous."

The lady in the long blue dress walks from behind the Christmas tree. It's her—Ma Gillick! Paddy waves his arms. She hurries across the stage to the piano without even a glance in his direction. Santa Claus then rushes out bellowing: *HO! HO! HO!*

The audience seated in chairs stand, everyone clapping and cheering. Santa dashes to the center of the stage, drops his big red sack, and takes a deep bow. Then, turning to the Santa kids, raising his arms over his head, he waits. The auditorium gets quiet. Santa looks to the piano player. Ma Gillick smiles back. She strikes a note. Santa swings his arms down. The Santa kids burst into song:

Deck the halls with boughs of holly,
Fa la la la la, la la la la.
'Tis the season to be jolly,
Fa la la la la, la la la la.

Paddy looks once again up at Joey, who is now watching the Santa kids, not him. He turns back, his mind softly taunting: *You left him flat, your best friend. Stupido—stupido.*

Don we now our gay apparel,
Fa la la, fa la la, la la la.
Troll the ancient Yuletide carol,
Fa la la la la, la la la la.

He watches Santa and the singers: *Stupido! Stupido!* The word racing through his head. Heaving a deep sigh, he pushes up from the seat with a clanging of the long brace on the seat in front of him.

"Hay, quiet." The girl next to him glances over.

"Sorry."

Stepping from the great seat, he turns his back on the stage and starts back up the aisle.

See the blazing Yule before us,
Fa la la la la, la la la la.
Strike the harp and join the chorus.
Fa la la la la, la la la la.

"Sorry, sorry." He apologizes to angry looking faces as he moves along, seatback to seatback.

Follow me in merry measure,
Fa la la la la, la la la la.
While I tell of Yuletide treasure,
Fa la la la la, la la la la.

Near the top of the aisle, he tries to move on faster. Suddenly, the feeble left foot catches a seat leg. Stumbling forward, he reaches madly for the next seatback—and misses. The steel braces hit the wood floor—a thunder clap to Paddy's ears—the rest of him following with a dull thud.

Fast away the old year passes,
Fa la la la la la, la la la la.
Hail the new, ye lads and lasses,
Fa la la la la, la la la la.

"What-the-fuck!" a boy growls, looking down at him from his seat.

"Didn't mean it," Paddy mumbles, sprawled in the aisle, mortified.

"Pitiful little twerp," the boy sneers.

Blessed-Virgin-Mary-Mother-of-God—make me disappear! Paddy prays to himself. Giggling heads all around now gaping at him.

Johnny Cant then appears, squatting beside him and motioning for the gigglers to stop. "Ya okay, Champ?"

"Yes," Paddy moans, as he is lifted to his feet.

Johnny Cant takes his hand, and they walk side-by-side up the aisle, Paddy with his head down feeling all the eyes gazing at the *pitiful little twerp.* The voices of the Santa kids rise. The piano pounds:

Sing we joyous, all together!
Fa la la, fa la la, la la la!
Heedless of the wind and weather!
Fa la la la la, la—la—la—la!

When they reach the *vegetable cart,* the auditorium is booming with cheers and applause. Joey is clapping away, his eyes fixed on the stage where the Santa Clause and the Santa kids are taking bows.

"You can see as good from up here, Joey," Paddy says loudly, but timidly, while Johnny Cant boosts him over the wooden sides of the *vegetable cart.*

As Santa Clause rushes across the stage—HO! HO! HO!—and disappears behind the Christmas tree, Joey turns to Paddy, yelling, "Have a nice trip?"

"What?" Paddy flops into the *vegetable cart.*

"Did you have a nice trip?" Joey says, as the auditorium quiets. "That's a joke—*stupido!*"

"Oh." Paddy all of a sudden gets it.

And they both break up in loud laughter, Johnny Cant, too.

"Silence! Or you'll have to leave!" Out of the blue, Nurse McCormick is beside the *vegetable cart* looking nastier than ever.

"And you," she shakes her finger at Johnny Cant. "You should know better!"

"Yes, ma'am." He flashes his gold teeth at her.

Joey and Paddy eye each other, red faced and tight-lipped, holding back their laughter.

"Better settle down," Johnny Cant warns them when Nurse McCormick rushes off. "Or she'll likely toss us out."

They then watch quietly as the walking Santa kids leave the stage and fill the empty front rows of seats while those in wheelchairs move to the back of the stage. When everyone is all settled, a priest in a long, white robe comes from behind the Christmas tree and goes to the center of the stage where he begins telling the story of Jesus being born in a manger.

When he is well into the story, Joey calls quietly to Johnny Cant. "We gotta go."

"Yeah, boy?" He steps over from his place against the wall.

"We gotta go. I peed myself," Joey mutters.

"Sure. We're outta here," Johnny Cant says softly.

"What—go?" Paddy looks with alarm at Johnny Cant, then to Joey. "We can't go, Joey. It's not over. There's more, lots more."

Joey shakes his head. "I have to leave—now."

"No. Please." Paddy turns back to Johnny Cant. "We can't! What about the candy?"

"Wanna stay, stay…ya can walk ya self right back down there." Johnny Cant nods his head toward the empty seat while sliding his hands under Paddy's arms as if to lift him from the *vegetable cart.*

"No! Wait—I'll go." Paddy shoves his hands away.

With that, Johnny Cant quickly maneuvers the *vegetable cart* from under the balcony and hurries it down the side aisle and out from the auditorium. Then, part way down Broadway, he slows down and steers them up in front of a window and stops. "Be right back," he says and sprints back down Broadway and disappears into the auditorium.

Paddy and Joey sit quietly staring out at the snow going gray in the late afternoon light. Sad faces in cockeyed Santa hats stare back at them in the window glass.

"Paddy," Joey says softly.

"Yeah," he grumbles, not turning to him.

"Does it smell bad?"

"What?"

"My pee, does it smell?"

"Kind-a."

"You know, I really didn't want to leave." Joey sighs. "I just go sometimes—can't stop it."

"Ah, it's okay. It really don't smell so bad," Paddy says, looking at him.

"You sure?" Joey grins uneasily.

"Yeah."

"We had a good time, anyway. Didn't we?" Joey perks up a little.

"Yeah. It was fun." Paddy smirks. "Except for my *nice trip.*"

"And what about come back again next fall."

They laugh together. And Joey is right back to his usual self—talking away, in his tough-guy, Brooklyn accent.

"Wanna hear about the best stickball game ever?" he asks.

"Sure," Paddy answers, happy they're best friends again.

"Well, it was last summer, on the feast day of St. Rosalina. She's the saint that watches over Sicily. That's in Italy. Lots of people in his neighborhood are from there, like Nonna and grandpa too, but he's dead. Anyway, it's a real special day with a huge parade up on the avenue, big party at the church, and a big stickball game.

"The stickball game, it's against guys from Queens. Irish guys. A money game where everyone bets on who'll win—and with pitching, not *fungo*. The street is blocked off with garbage cans. No cars allowed, except for the Irish guys. They're allowed to park down at the end of the street. Everyone in the neighborhood is out, mostly sitting on the stoops drinking beer. And Nonna and me are at the front window. Below us, Papa, Uncle Louie, Uncle Ralph, and the old bocce guys are sitting on chairs lined up along the curb.

"It's a terrific game—close all the way. Then, in the seventh inning, score tied six to six, and Tony, our best hitter, he comes to bat. On the first pitch, he smacks a three-sewer-homer—the only one of the game. Everyone is up on their feet cheering and yelling—'what a fuckin' shot'—as Tony trots around the bases waving and making funny bows.

"As our next guy then is coming to bat, the pitcher calls over to Tony—'lucky hit mother-fucker.' Tony, who is talking to the bocce guys, he picks up a bat and walks coolly up to the pitcher who has turned away from him. 'Fuck you *mick,*' he yells and whacks the Irish guy in the head with the bat. Down he goes. And boy—did the shit hit the fan!

"Our guys and the Irish guys start throwing punches and swinging bats. Tony is right in the middle of it all—he's our best fighter, too. It was great! But, then Nonna, she got really excited and went and screwed it all up. Leaning way out the window, she starts screaming down to Papa—*Fermarlo! Fermarlo! Fermarlo!* That's 'stop them' in Italian.

"Papa looks up, waves for her to get back inside. Then, along with Uncle Ralph, Uncle Louie, and the bocce guys, he goes and breaks up the fight."

"Paddy," Joey shakes his head disappointedly, "it would-a been better than the greatest fight ever, except for Nonna butting in. She thinks she's the boss of everyone. Anyway, they start the game again, and as I knew they would, our team wins, eight to seven. And all the players shake hands like best friends. Uncle Ralph then goes around collecting the betting money from the Irish guys, and after that the Irish guys, they head for their cars as if the game over: they lost, paid up, that's it.

"But that wasn't the end. When they're halfway down the block, one of the Irish guys turns around yelling—'ya only won, Tony, because ya fuckin' sly-rapped our best pitcher.' Tony, right away, he grabs a bat and heads for the Irish guys—with all our stickball guys and other guys from stoops following him.

"The Irish guys all stop. I'm thinking they're gonna fight. They're nuts. They'll get killed. Then, what do they do?" Joey laughs, his eyes glowing real bright and happy.

"They turn tail and run for their cars—scared shitless. Our guys take off after them—shouting 'chicken shit' and throwing garbage cans at their cars speeding away! It was something, Paddy!" Joey laughs again, all excited. "Really something!"

"Yeah—wow, really something," Paddy laughs with him. "That's your best story."

"Then," Joey continues, nodding his head indicating there's more. "Tony came upstairs, lifted me up on his shoulders, and took me up the avenue to the parade—he always does things like that. And everyone tells us how it was the greatest stickball game ever, saying—'but ya should-a kicked the shit out of the Irish fucks'—and..."

"Yoe!" Johnny Cant calls out.

He's jogging toward them. Close behind him is Santa Claus, lugging his big sack. When they get to the *vegetable cart,* Santa is huffing and his white beard is twisted out of place. He looks at Paddy, winks, and quickly straightens the whiskers. Paddy smiles thinking: *It's Dr. Ingersoll, that's for sure.*

Santa then reaches into his sack—booming, "HO! HO! HO!"—and he pulls out two candy boxes, blue with white stars like last year.

"Merry Christmas, boys!" he says in a deep voice, handing one box to Joey and the other to Paddy. "May God bless you both!"

"Thank you, Santa," they say together.

"Hold on, Mr. Claus," Johnny Cant says as Santa picks up his sack. "Don't be stingy, man. These is the best two dudes in this here reconstruction home," adding with a make believe pout, "and what 'bout me?"

Santa looks carefully at Joey and then at Paddy, his eyes crinkling as if making sure they really are *the two best dudes in this here reconstruction home.* Booming once more— "HO! HO! HO!"—he digs into his sack coming up with three more candy boxes.

"Again, Merry Christmas, boys," he says, sounding now like Dr. Ingersoll, as he hands over the second boxes.

He tosses the third box to Johnny Cant, who whisks it from the air with one hand.

"Thanks, Santa," Paddy and Joey say, once more in unison with Johnny Cant joining in.

Swinging his bag to his shoulder, Dr.-Santa-Ingersoll walks away, calling out in his Santa voice, "Merry Christmas to all! And to all a good night!"

CHAPTER XIX

Joey's Family Visits
December 25, 1941
Day: Four Hundred and Sixty-one

When Nurse Kelly arrives, carrying two packages neatly wrapped in Christmas paper, Paddy and Joey are already up sitting in Joey's bed practicing writing with fountain pens each received as gifts from Nurse Edelstein, along with bottles of blue ink and a writing book.

"Put your pens away," Nurse Kelly says briskly. "You don't want to stain what I have here for you."

They quickly cap their pens. Paddy places pen and writing book into his desk where he's sitting. Joey stretching over in his bed and puts his on his nightstand. Nurse Kelly then hands each a package and watches as they tear into the green wrapping to uncover white, V-neck swatters.

"Woven from fine Irish wool by me Sister Nora herself in her shop back home in Bulmullet," Nurse Kelly says cheerfully.

Looking over their gifts, they thank her—each secretly wishing they would get toys instead of things like a pen and now a sweater.

"You can put them on if you like. I'll be back after breakfast."

As they struggle into their new garments, heavy and warm, Mr. Martin arrives carrying a breakfast tray in each hand and a long rolled up paper tucked under one arm. Setting the trays before them, he then steps to the center of the room.

"Wrote a Christmas poem for ya," he says with his gummy smile.

Paddy and Joey watch with anticipation as he takes the paper from under his arm and unrolls it; it's about the size of a pillowcase with words printed on it in large, neat red letters. Holding the paper below his chin, one hand grasping it at the top and the other at the bottom, he gives Paddy and Joey each a gummy smile and then recites:

Merry Christmas to you all,
To my two buddies,
One short, one tall,
That's the greeting of the year,
From Santa Claus,
And his reindeer.

Paddy laughs, applauding enthusiastically when he finishes, "That's a great poem Mr. Martin."

Joey wrinkles his nose, as if smelling something bad. He doesn't clap, and says nothing. Looking at him, Paddy thinks: *Bet he don't like it because he's the short buddy and I'm the tall one.* Mr. Martin smiles at Paddy, turns away, and limps off with a quiet, "Merry Christmas."

Soon after he leaves, Nurse Kelly returns with a box wrapped in brown paper. "Here you go, Paddy—a package from Albany," she announces. "But you may want to wait an' open it until Joey's family comes with his presents. Should be here soon."

"No, I'll do it now," Paddy says rising from the desk and toddling over to take the box from her.

"Open here by me," Joey says from his bed.

"Sure." Paddy places the box on Joey's bed and drags himself up on to the end of it.

Sitting with the box between himself and Joey, he pulls off the mailing paper to reveal Christmas wrapping underneath, green trees on silver paper and tied neatly with a red ribbon. He admires it for moment thinking: *Kate wrapped it.*

"What ya waiting for—open it," Joey orders impatiently.

Paddy removes the ribbon and carefully undoes the wrapping, letting it fall to the floor, revealing a brown cardboard box. He opens it. On top is an envelope. He quickly tucks it under his shirt. Below that are four Hershey Bars and a large bag of jelly beans. He tosses one of the Hershey Bars to Joey who quickly slides it under his pillow. The rest of the candy Paddy places behind him, out of Joey's reach. At the bottom of the box is as a second box, a picture of a pistol on it.

"Box says it's a *Hubley Champ Fifty Shot Repeater.*" Joey reaches for it. "Now we got a rifle and a pistol,"

"It's mine. The rifle, too." Paddy pulls the box away.

He lifts the pistol box out of the packaging. Opening it, he removes a small, silver pistol. While Paddy admires its pearl handle, with a red star on it, Joey takes the pistol box. Searching inside, he finds two boxes of caps.

"Five rolls. Fifty caps per roll," Joey says, reading the wording on one of the cap boxes. "Wow, that's 500 shots in all. Let's see the fuckin' gun a second."

"Hold on," Paddy says, fiddling with the pistol to release a pop-up place on the top of the handle.

"That's where the caps go," Joey says, opening one of the boxes of caps. "Come on, let me see it."

Paddy reluctantly hands him the great pistol. Joey loads a roll of caps in the pop-up place and closes it. Then holding the gun over his head, he squeezes his eyes shut, and he pulls the trigger:

BANG!

Their hearts jump from the ear-piercing blast. Their faces then beaming as they watch the smoke drift up from the pistol. Joey fires again:

BANG! BANG! BANG!

"Jaysus-Mary-an'-Joseph," Nurse Kelly shouts, bursting into the room. "Yer'ill be wakin' the dead if you don't burn the place down first."

She rushes over and takes the pistol from Joey, studies it for a second, pops open the cap place, and removes the remaining ammunition.

"Give me the rest of 'em," she demands, looking harshly at Joey.

He hesitates.

"Joey!"

He hands her the open box of caps.

"Any more?"

"No," Joey lies.

"Now, listen up," she says, placing the caps in her uniform pocket, 'Tis Christmas day. I'm off for the afternoon. Joey, yer to take a nap before yer folks arrive. And, Paddy, into yer own bed. You can do with a bit of rest, too."

When Paddy is settled in his bed, Nurse Kelly places the pistol and his candies under the desk top. As she is about to leave, he says quietly, "Will you help me read my letter."

"What letter?"

"Was in the Christmas package along with the candies the pistol box."

"Sure, let me see it."

Paddy pulls the envelope from his shirt, hands it to her, and she sits on the bed next to him.

"You want to open it?"

"No. And you read it all please—and like whisper," he murmurs, glancing over at Joey, "so he doesn't hear."

"You can read it yerself," she whispers back.

"Please, that will take too long and maybe I'd miss some."

"Okay," she says softly and carefully opens the envelope and slides out the letter.

"Ah, again your dad's lovely writing." She unfolds the two pages and quietly reads:

14 December 1941

Dear Son,

We are all settled in Albany now. The handyman job at the college is fine. I am still learning the ropes. Kate, Little Billy, and your mom are well.

I am sorry we will not be able to see you for Christmas. That is because we have no car. Coming home from visiting you on your birthday, we had an accident. We ran into some ice and the car went off the road. Everyone is fine except your mom got a world-class shiner. It is about gone now. However, the car was wrecked. Maybe after the holidays we will come by bus. Kate is sitting at the table with me. She wants to tell you about little Billy.

Hi! Paddy,

Guess what happened yesterday morning. Little Billy disappeared. It was after Pop went to work. Mom and me, we looked in all his hiding places. Under the crib. Behind the coach. In the cabinet with the pots and pans. He wasn't anywhere! And Mom got real upset.

Then stinky Ms. Beck came down from upstairs. She said she could see little Billy from her bedroom window. He was down the block playing on a snow pile—and only in his diaper!

I ran and got him. He didn't even want to leave the snow pile. He wasn't cold, he said, and wanted to keep playing. I had to drag him back to the house. When we got home, Mom scolded him (just a little). After that, we all laughed. It was real funny.

School is good and everything else. Pop said he killed all the rats. But at night, I still hear them sometimes. Hope you like the candies. I picked them out. Here's Pop again

Merry Christmas

Love Kate XXXOOO.

Well, son, I hope the gift is a good one and you have fun with it. Your mom says not to eat the candies all at once. She sends her love.

Have a Happy Christmas,

Your Father.

When she finishes the letter, Paddy quietly weeps a little, moaning. "They're not coming for Christmas. Thought maybe they would as a surprise."

"Were they not just here for your birthday?" Nurse Kelly gives him a hug and places the letter in his desk. "Cheer up now. Yer'ill have a grand time with Joey and his family."

* * *

Joey's family arrived just before lunchtime, except for Tony. He's on a troop ship. "Going to kill Nazis," according to Joey. Like Joey, his mom, grandma Nonna, and his sisters, Marcella and Nina, talk all the time, sometimes *Italian*. But Joey's dad doesn't say much. He just sits by the sink reading the *Daily News*.

They brought food, lots of it. And Joey's dad *borrowed* a table from the doctor's conference room. Paddy laughed to himself, wishing he had *borrowed* Mr. Bones as well. The women put out the food. And then Joey's dad said grace:

Lord bless this precious bread,
Bless the goodness we are eating,
Bless our children, particularly Tony now off to war,
And our whole family.
Amen.

Joey's mom then added, "Lord, whose ways are beyond understanding, we pray for the elevation to heaven the soul of our beloved Rocco where the Master of mercy will care for him for all time. We ask this through Christ our Lord. God bless Tony. Amen."

There were all different things to eat—spaghetti, sausage and peppers, various cheeses, salad, bread that Nonna has sprinkled with oil, and even things that, to Paddy, looked like little octopuses.

"They're squid—*calamari*," Joey's mom told him as he stood gaping at them.

He didn't take any.

They also brought a big chocolate cake, bottles of soda, and wine for Joey's dad. Nonna and Joey's mom had some, too.

Then when everybody finished eating, Joey opened his presents. First, was *The Sporting News Official Record Book*. "Got everything about every baseball since the beginning of the game. Best present ever!" Joey said, leafing happily threw it.

Next was a shoe box full of lead soldiers. While Joey fished through the box looking at them, Joey's mom explained to Paddy that they are very special. "Tony bought them one a week when he had his paper route. And since he's a soldier himself now, God protect him, he said Joey could have them."

* * *

Now, it's relatively quiet. Joey's mom and Nonna are cleaning up. Marcella and Nina are by Joey's bed. He's reading softly to them from *The Sporting News Record Book*. Paddy is at his desk playing with the cap pistol and wondering to himself if the Rocco Joey's mom prayed for is the same Rocco in the iron lung—the one Joey told him would die.

"Hay, Paddy," Joey calls. "Wanna play with my soldiers?"

"Yeah. Thanks."

Paddy slides the cap pistol under the desktop. As he shuffles over to Joey's bed, he sees Marcella and Nina are smiling at him, somewhat mischievously.

"There are twenty-seven soldiers here." Joey hands him the cigar box.

Taking the box, Paddy asks quietly, "Did Rocco in the iron lung die?"

"Yeah, last week," Joey answers with a shrug of his shoulders.

Then, tapping the cigar box with his finger, Joey repeats, "Twenty-seven soldiers in here," and adds handing him the box, "and there'll be twenty-seven soldiers when I get them back. Right?"

"Sure." Paddy nods.

Sitting on his bed, Paddy rummages through the cigar box. There are all different kinds of soldiers—some standing at attention, others shooting rifles and pistols, two firing machine guns, even one playing a bugle and another a drum.

While he lays them out on top of the covers, Marcella slides up on his bed beside him. She's nice, very pretty, too, with long dark hair and big brown eyes. She starts asking him questions: what his dad does; where he lives; does he have sisters and brothers. Things like that. Paddy answers as they place the soldiers in two lines across the bed, armies facing each other. After a little while, Marcella takes a lipstick and mirror from a small pocketbook. Looking in the mirror, she carefully applies the lipstick, bright red.

"Come here...lean toward me. Close your eyes," she says when finished.

Paddy bends toward her, eyes closed. She kisses his cheek—a lovely quiver runs through him.

"Okay, open your eyes," she says pulling away. "Was that nice?"

"Yes," he answers shyly, his face flushed and feeling warm.

Marcella then puts her lipstick and mirror away and starts telling Paddy about being a cheerleader and about how high school is better than elementary school because you don't stay in one classroom all day. He's hardly listening, just moving the soldiers around hoping she'll kiss him again.

Suddenly, the silence of the room vanishes:

BANG! BANG!

The blasts startle Paddy, but right away he knows the source. Then again:

BANG! BANG! BANG!

He turns to Joey. Smoke is curling up from the barrel of the cap pistol, which is pointed at him. With a one-sided smile, Joey fires away once more:

BANG! BANG! BANG! BANG!

All at once, the room erupts: Marcella crying out, "Joey, ya got me," as she slides from Paddy's bed rolling across the floor; Nina, standing beside Joey, bending over laughing uncontrollably; Joey's mom shouting, "Stop! Joey! Stop!" while leaping from her chair; Nonna, arms waving, screaming *fermarlo! fermarlo;* Joey's dad throwing down the *Daily News* and rushing to take the pistol from Joey.

There is then a rapping on the door, a sharp rapping. The room goes silent; hardly a sound, just the radiator hissing softly.

"Yes!" Joey's dad says loudly, placing the pistol behind his back.

The door slowly opens. A nurse, one Paddy doesn't know, pokes her head into the room.

"Hi, I'm Nurse Slone. Everything all right here?" She sniffs the air. "Do I smell smoke?"

"Yes, we're fine. Just playing a game and blowing out some candles," Marcella says, grinning up at the nurse from the floor.

"Yes, yes, it's my birthday," Joey's mom says very calmly. "Come in, won't you, Nurse...Nurse Slone? Have something. Some wonderful chocolate cake?"

"No thank you. Won't disturb you all. Sounds like you are having a very Merry Christmas. And happy birthday to you, Mrs. Lombardi."

"Thank you." She smiles with a little bow.

With a wave of her hand, Nurse Slone pulls the door shut.

Once again it's quiet for a moment.

Then, in a loud whisper Joey says, "Mama, pass me that piece of *wonderful* chocolate cake."

The room erupts with laughter, with even Joey's dad joining in—Paddy, too.

* * *

That night when Nurse Slone leaves turning off the lights, Joey asks from his bed," Did ya have a good time, Paddy?"

"It was great. You shooting the pistol and all." Paddy chuckles as he snuggles down under his covers.

"I bet you liked Marcella kissing you best—didn't you? I saw it."

"How did you get the gun without anyone seeing?" Paddy answers, not wanting to talk about Marcella's wonderful kiss, it being so very special.

"It was easy. A set-up," Joey laughs quietly. "Marcella gets into your bed. She talks a little. She tells you to close your eyes. And, while she gives ya a kiss, Nina sneaks the gun from your desk."

"What!" Paddy sits up looking angrily at Joey who's all hunkered down in his covers. "Marcella, she was nice to me—only to trick me?"

"Relax." Joey grins at him. "She really thinks you're cool. Anyway, ya still got lipstick on your cheek."

"That was a dirty trick, Joey!" Paddy says, rubbing his cheek with the sleeve of his nightshirt.

"Ah, go to sleep, Paddy. We was only having fun."

Paddy slides down in his bed feeling sad--*stupido*. He says his Mom's prayer, makes the *Sign-of-the-Cross* on his legs, and kisses the holy medal. Closing his eyes, he rolls over on his stomach and rocks his head into the pillow unable to stop thinking of Marcella's kiss—the lovely quiver again races through him.

* * *

The rasping coughing wakes Paddy. In the dim moonlight, he sees Nurse Slone beside Joey's bed.

"What's wrong with Joey?" he calls groggily to her.

"Go back to sleep, Paddy. It's the middle of the night," she answers and pulls the curtain around Joey's bed.

Paddy snuggles back down under the covers and turns on his tummy listening to Joey coughing. After a while, Nurse Slone leaves the room for what seems like a long time, Joey coughing all the while. She at last returns with a doctor. Not Doctor Strasburg or Doctor Ingersoll, someone else. They go behind the curtain. Joey's coughing soon stops. Paddy rocks his head drifting into dreamless sleep.

CHAPTER XX

The Operation
January 2, 1942
Day: Four Hundred and Nine

"Remember me?"

Paddy turns his head to see a nurse walking toward him. He scoots up on the cold steel table for a better look.

"Uh-huh. Nurse McCormick." A sour taste creeps up into his throat. He swallows hard.

"That's correct!" She grins, showing her big teeth.

"I'm going to throw up," Paddy groans.

"You haven't eaten anything, have you?" she asks sharply and removes his blanket.

"No. Johnny Cant took me here before Mr. Martin brought my breakfast."

"Good. You'll be fine. Let's get you undressed. Sit up. Lift your arms."

"What's happening?" Paddy sobs as he sits up and swallows back more sour taste.

"No whining like last time." She slips his nightgown from under him and pulls it over his head. "Now, lie down."

As he flops back on to the silver table, she tugs at his underpants.

"No!" he shouts lifting his head and reaching to stop her. "Please!"

"Oh! Such modesty." She pushes his hand away, pulls the underpants off, and places a towel across his hips.

"Better, now?" She grins.

"Yes." He holds down the towel.

Covering him then with a sheet, Nurse McCormick walks away.

Paddy closes his eyes, praying silently: *Blessed Virgin Mary please don't let them give me casts again.* He hears clicking footsteps coming toward him.

"Hello, there."

Opening his eyes, he sees Dr. Strasburg smiling down at him, his caterpillar mustache scrunching up against his nostrils like it's trying to get back where it came from.

"And how are we today?"

"You giving me casts again?" Paddy asks, sitting up.

"We're going to fix it so you can walk better. And, yes, you will have a cast on your left leg for a while—remember Dr. Ingersoll?" He motions toward the end of the table.

Paddy glances at Dr. Ingersoll.

"Hi there." The doctor waves.

"You don't have to fix me," Paddy says, looking back at Dr. Strasburg. "I'm walking good now. And I ride my tricycle real good, too—all the way to the kitchen, and..."

"Yes, yes, we know. Lie down," the doctor replies.

He slowly rests back on the table. Dr. Strasburg switches on the overhead light, removes the sheet—Paddy holding the towel tight down over his privates—and gently moves the *flaccid* left foot, up and down and side to side.

"We'll transplant the *extensor hallucis longus* and *extensor digitorum longus.*" He addresses Dr. Ingersoll. "And then we will perform an *arthrodesis* of the *interphalangeal* joint of the big toe so the bones grow solidly together."

Paddy raises his head, tears filling his eyes, and tugs on Dr. Strasburg sleeve. "Ma Gillick, she says I'm a whole lot better. I'm going home soon."

Nurse McCormick lowers her face to his, her nose bumping his ear, and with cigarette breath she whispers, "We don't want to be acting like big sissy now, do we?"

Paddy drops his head back with a thud and whispers back, trying hard not to sound fag-ie, "*Fuck* you."

"What? What-did-you-say?" she sputters, her head jerking from him as if he had poked her in the eye.

Dr. Strasburg turns to her. "Something wrong?"

She looks at the doctor, her face fiery red, her eyes widened, glaring, "He..." She hesitates, turning back to Paddy. "No, nothing, doctor."

Then, as if out of nowhere, a deep voice comes from behind Paddy's head. "Young fellow."

He stretches his neck and looks back to see an upside-down head peering at him, its face hidden behind large glasses and a white mask.

"I'm Doctor Schwartz. I bet you're a good counter."

"Yes, Nurse Edelstein said..."

"That's good. I'm going to place a small cover over your nose and mouth. It won't hurt. Stay still."

A cup-like device, smelling of rubbing alcohol, slides over his face.

"Close your eyes. Relax. And now count to ten to yourself. Slowly, slowly—breathe easily."

Paddy lets his chin fall forward. He counts, "One... two...three...four..." while looking up at Dr. Strasburg stroking his caterpillar and Nurse McCormick beside him, her eyes narrowed and mouth turned down.

Tears roll down his cheeks and into his ears. They tickle. "Five...six...seven..."

* * *

"You awake?" Paddy opens his eyes. Nurse Edelstein is leaning over him.

"Here, take this and drink some water."

He raises his head. It's dark, no moonlight, just a crack of light from the doorway. He swallows the pill. She holds a straw to his mouth. Sipping, he sees the white cast floating over the bed.

"Go back to sleep," Nurse Edelstein says softly, stroking his head.

He closes his eyes and dreams:

Flying above heavy clouds,
Suddenly an opening.
Far below two snowmen are sitting on a bench.
He lets up on the stick. Gliding down.
The snowmen look up.
He goes faster.
One snowman cries out,
"Pray, darlin'. You must pray to the Blessed Virgin Mary. She'll listen!"
The second snowman shouts,
"Do your pop proud, son—get the blewdy legs fixed."
Faster! Faster! Tingling now, tingling all over.
They're melting!
"Pray, darlin'…"
Melting! Melting!
"Do your pop proud…"
They splash down.
"Mommy! Mommy!"
Paddy cries out in silence.

CHAPTER XXI

Despair and Toughness
January 3, 1942
Day: Four Hundred and Seventy

"Good mornin', Paddy."

The dream is still in his head as he awakes.

"They melted," he mumbles.

"Who's that, that melted?" Nurse Kelly asks, smiling down at him.

"Mom and Pop—they did. They melted."

"Sure, 'tis a dream you had. Time to wake up—a lovely day. A glorious sun at long last is payin' us a visit."

Paddy lifts his head. He sees it, the dreadful cast. That's no dream. It's there suspended by a harness above the bed.

"*She—she* didn't listen," he groans, throwing his head back on his pillow, tears bursting from his eyes.

"Who didn't listen to what?"

"She!"

"Who? What's wrong, child?"

"She! She!" he shrieks, pounding his fists into the bed. "Shit! Shit! Shit!"

"Now stop that! An' mind your language," Nurse Kelly says sternly as she steadies the cast swaying from the outburst.

Paddy slides up on his elbows shouting "Look! Look—my leg!"

"Calm down, child—calm down."

"I'll never walk again!" He throws himself back on to the bed, thrashing side-to-side. "I was doing good! Real good—and going home soon. Now look! Look what they did!"

"Easy, Paddy, settle down," Nurse Kelly says gently.

"Everyone—everyone hates me!" He stops moving and screams. "You, too. You hate me!"

"Sure, we all love you. An' with the help of God, yer'ill soon be up an' about—better than ever. But you must take hold of yerself now."

"No! No! No!" he shouts, eyes pressed shut, head and shoulders rocking side-to-side. "I hate you! I hate you!"

"Stop! Stop that bouncing about—you'll be hurtin' yerself!" Nurse Kelly shouts, her two hands now trying to steady the cast bouncing in its sling.

"I hate you! I hate Dr. Strasburg—that ugly Nurse McCormick!" he screams, tossing fitfully. "And I hate—I hate that—that stupid *Blessed Virgin Mary*. *She didn't—she* never listened!"

"Jaysus-Mary-an'-Joseph!" Nurse Kelly gasps, the cast jumping from her grasp. "What a terrible, terrible thing to say! Now stop! Stop! That's it! Enough's—enough!"

He feels the sharp sting of her hand across his face. He freezes. His eyes spring open.

Nurse Kelly—face scarlet—is glaring down at him, hand raised ready to strike again.

Then, a singsong voice, "I hate you. I hate everyone. So, I'll be off to the garden to eat worms."

Nurse Kelly spins her head to the door. Paddy is up on to his elbows. Ma Gillick walks into the room.

"Dear God! Martha—yer're not a minute too soon," Nurse Kelly gasps catching a breath. "He's been a holy terror—screechin' the place down—an' blasphemin' like a thing possessed!"

Ma Gillick strolls to the foot of Paddy's bed. She looks crossly at him for a long moment.

"A *holy terror* is he?" She turns to Nurse Kelly.

Paddy lays back and closes his eyes, his heart thumping in his ears.

"Ach—indeed," Nurse Kelly replies, softly now.

A moment later, Paddy feels a cover being pulled over him. A cool cloth then strokes his face. He opens his eyes.

Nurse Kelly smiles at him. "I'll be back later to give you a proper freshenin' up."

She turns away, adjusting her nurse cap, toppled to one side, and walks with Ma Gillick to the door. As they talk quietly, Paddy hears only one word clearly—*Joey*.

He looks to Joey's bed. It's empty, only a gray mattress and uncovered pillow. Joey's gone!

Rising up, he shouts, "Where's Joey at?"

Nurse Kelly glances at him, quickly turns away, and walks from the room.

"Nurse Kelly, where's Joey?" he calls after her as Ma Gillick comes toward him.

"Where's Joey?" he repeats, quietly, looking worriedly at Ma Gillick.

"He's gone," she answers.

"Home to Brooklyn?"

"Yes, well..." a trace of uncertainly crosses her face "to Brooklyn."

"Joey's my best friend, you know." Paddy rests back on his bed as Ma Gillick comes up beside him. "Now, I have no one to play with—and a stupid cast again. Can't walk. Can't ride my bike—or anything anymore." He raises his voice, "It ain't fair."

"Will have none of that," she responds in her no-nonsense voice. You are a bit of a mess right now," she says. "Still, you have little cause to throw such a fit as you did."

"But my leg! Look!" He shakes his finger at the dreadful cast. "See. Everyone does what they want to me! Everyone!"

"In a way, yes, that's true. Still, no amount of yelling and pounding will change anything. Tantrums won't make your cast disappear, or your polio go away, or in any way make things better for you. Acting out as you did is destructive. You about frightened Nurse Kelly to death. Such outbursts are not nice at all, and they make you look, well—feeble, weak."

"I'm not that. I'm strong. Mr. Cooney says so." Paddy sobs.

"You are strong and getting stronger, both in the pool and in my clinic. But I'm talking about something different than your physical strength."

She sits on the bed beside him. "Have you ever heard Joey complaining, never mind behaving as badly as you just did?"

"No." He shakes his head, wishing she'd just go away.

"Why wouldn't he?"

"Just wouldn't." He pouts.

"Why?"

"Don't know."

"Well, I'll tell you why. He's tough."

"He's from the toughest neighborhood in Brooklyn. He tells me all about it. And he can talk tough, too. "

"You don't have to be from a tough neighborhood and be a tough talker to be tough where Joey is really tough. He's tough here." She taps her forehead with her finger. "Tough inside his head."

"Joey has a tube inside his head," Paddy says brightly, wanting somehow to change the subject.

"Are you listening to me? Look at me." she says, staring into his eyes, unsmiling.

"Yes ma'am." He looks at her, feeling calmer.

"People who are tough, Joey-tough, control themselves—their emotions, their bad tempers."

"It just came out," he moans, looking sorrowfully at her.

"Just came out? When I hurt you during your physiotherapy, do you yelp? No, you do not. You don't let it—*just come out*."

"That's because of the *no yelping rule*."

"Well, we have got ourselves another rule now. The *be tough rule*. It says *no destructive emotions*—emotions that hurt people, as you hurt Nurse Kelly. "

"I didn't hurt her," Paddy protests. "She hurt me. She hit me."

"You did hurt Nurse Kelly. You upset her very much because she had to resort to striking you so you wouldn't injure yourself. She would never do anything like that otherwise. And you made her sad, very sad, with the things you said. Do you understand?"

She brushes back his hair.

"I guess."

"So now, putting the *be tough rule* into practice. Even when you heart is aching something terrible, as it was a few minutes ago—no more tantrums. That's finished. Right." She looks him in the eye again.

"Yes. No more *tantrums,*" he moans, turning his head away.

"Keep looking at me," she demands. He turns back. "Also, you don't take your misfortune, your having polio, out on others by being nasty and angry or by forever feeling sorry for yourself and spreading that gloom about like salt on ice-cream. It leaves a bad taste. If you do you'll have few real friends. People just won't want to have much to do with you."

She pauses for a moment and again brushes back Paddy's hair saying, "The *be tough rule* is a difficult rule to follow, more so than the *no yelping rule*. The hurt that causes yelps usually goes away far faster than the hurt that causes sadness and heart aches. Still, you're going to follow the *be tough rule*—right?"

"I'll try," Paddy mumbles.

"Try!" She looks sharply at him.

"I will," he quickly corrects himself, wishing really hard she'll now go away.

To his dismay, Ma Gillick continues softly. "You know, Paddy, bad, hurtful things happen to everyone—things that discouraged us."

He rolls the pillow from behind his head and covers his face. Ma Gillick lifts it away.

"I want to go to sleep," Paddy whimpers, eyes drooping.

"Almost finished," she says, gently raising Paddy's head and returns the pillow it to where it belongs.

"Some bad and hurtful things," she places her hand lightly on the cast, "are clear to see. Others bad and hurtful things only doctors and nurses get to see—like the tube inside Joey's head that goes to his tummy. And some things, often the baddest and most hurtful of all, are invisible. They're hidden away inside the brain, the mind—out of sight. They can't be seen even by doctors."

"But not you, though. You don't get—bad things?"

"Oh, I do indeed." She playfully touches the tip of his nose. "End of lecture—now brighten up. Your cast will eventually be cut off and tossed in the garbage. Your legs will get stronger. You will be up and about in no time, walking and riding your tricycle again. And you will be going home."

He smiles weakly at her.

"But that all really depends on *you*. *You* must believe that by working hard and following our *rules—you* will make yourself better, even if bad and hurtful things may set you back some. Remember it's up to *you*—no one else, *you*."

Leaning over, she kisses his forehead. "You know, relying on yourself isn't so dreadful. There's certain fun, an excitement in it, and real joy in being able to say to yourself—*I did it*."

"Fun? How's it fun?" He responds pulling his covers up under his chin.

"You'll understand that better when you get older."

He sighs, feeling exhausted, the tantrum and lecture having sapped all his energy.

"Now, what's the new rule?"

"The be tough rule."

"And what does it say?"

"No *tantrums* and being mean—stuff like that."

"Fine," she smiles. "I'm going. But I'll see you again soon." She stands up from the bed.

"When?"

"Won't be long."

Walking toward the door, Ma Gillick stops and looks back at Paddy.

"And don't forget to tell Nurse Kelly you're sorry for upsetting her."

* * *

After she leaves, Paddy raises up looking at the ugly cast—the gleaming white *plaster-of-Paris* encasing his entire left leg, even his toes this time. He then unclasps the silver chain from his neck and winds it into a ball around the images of *Blessed Virgin Mary* and *Sacred Hear of Jesus.* Twisting his torso as far as he can toward the window, he tosses the holy medal:

Cling!

It strikes the wall above the hissing radiator and vanishes behind it. He turns back thinking what Joey would say, if he's not dead like cousin Rocco: *Good fuckin' shot Paddy. Ya got an arm like our best fielder Dixie Walker.*

CHAPTER XXII

The Sinking of the Vancouver
February 20, 1942
Day: Five Hundred and Eighteen

"Well, Paddy, we're going to see what that foot of yours looks like." Dr. Strasburg strolls up to him, followed by Blue Apron pushing her casting cart and behind her awful Nurse McCormick.

"The cast itches at the top," Paddy complains, sitting up on the steel casting room table.

"You know you shouldn't be scratching it," Nurse McCormick says sharply. She comes beside and slides his gown up to his knees. "It would itch less if you would control yourself."

"Now, what I'm going to do today," Dr. Strasburg says, "is cut *a window* in the cast over the top of your foot to see inside. If the incisions look good, I'll remove the stitches. Follow me?"

"Yes, Nurse Kelly told me," Paddy mumbles. "She said it wouldn't hurt."

"Now lie back on the table." Nurse McCormick commands. "I expect you'll behave not like last time."

"Can't I watch?" he asks Dr. Strasburg, ignoring her.

"No, lie back like I told you," Nurse McCormick answers for the doctor.

"We'll let him while I cut the window," Dr. Strasburg says, with a *we're buddies* wink at Paddy.

"As you wish, doctor," she replies.

Blue Apron positions her cart across the table from Dr. Strasburg. She removes a flat-end scissors from the top of it and hands it over to him.

"Don't move now, Paddy," Nurse McCormick says, holding the cast steady.

Paddy squeezes the table as the scissor blade slides between the cast and his little toe. It then cuts slowly along the side of his foot to his ankle, turns across to his other ankle, and moves down the other side of his foot to his big toe, carving a U.

Dr. Strasburg looks up at him. "This last part may hurt some."

Paddy nods, gripping the table harder.

The scissor continues slicing its way slowly across from his big toe back to the little one to close the top of the U. Paddy groans—not a yelp, though.

"So you see, Paddy," Dr. Strasburg says, handing the scissors back to Blue Apron who gives him a smaller one, "we now have the neat outline of the window. Let's say we open it."

With his fingers, he pries away the piece of cast, cuts away the bandage beneath the cutout, and peels it away. Paddy yelps as the gauze is removed, but not too loud.

The *window* opened, Paddy gapes at the three ugly incisions. One wide and purplish runs down the top of his foot. Another, thin and red, goes from his ankle to big toe. A third incision, also thin and red, cuts crosses the big toe. It has no toenail. Black shoelace-like stitches hold the cut together.

"What—what did you do to my foot?" He whimpers.

Placing his finger lightly on the purple cut, Dr. Strasburg says, "I fixed it so you can walk better. And I must say the incisions look excellent."

His finger pushes down.

"Ouch!" Paddy calls out. "That hurts!"

"None of that," growls Nurse McCormick giving his shoulder a nudge with her hand. "Now, lie down."

"Yes," Dr. Strasburg agrees. "Show's over."

Flopping back, Paddy pulls his arm across his face trying hard to hold back the tears, not wanting to be a *big sissy.*

"Now, young man, I'm going to start removing the stitches. It'll hurt some," Dr. Strasburg says.

"Nurse Kelly said it wouldn't." He sighs, peeking from under his arm.

Each scissor snip and tweezer pluck stings, stings badly. *Nurse Kelly didn't tell the truth,* Paddy moans to himself while pressing his arm hard against his eyes.

"That's it," Dr. Strasburg says after what to Paddy seemed forever.

Sliding up on his elbows, he watches as Nurse McCormick dabs drops of blood from the tiny stitch holes.

"Now," Dr. Strasburg grins at him from the foot of the table, "that wasn't too bad, was it?"

Paddy doesn't answer as he watches Nurse McCormick cover his scars with gauze. He then slides back on the table, hiding his eyes again and soon feels the cool damp *plaster-of-Paris* closing the *window.*

"All done now, Paddy. You can sit up," Dr. Strasburg's voice rings cheerfully. "Your foot looks very good, excellent."

"It doesn't. It's ugly," he mutters as he pushes himself up into a sitting position.

"Come now." The doctor steps from the end of the table and pats Paddy's head. "We'll soon be removing the entire cast—and for good."

Nurse McCormick, placing a sheet over his legs, whispers, "You were a pretty good boy this time—none of that sissy stuff and dirty language of yours."

He really wants to *curse her out*. He doesn't.

* * *

"Why so glum, chum," Johnny Cant asks as they head back to the room, *clip-clopping* along faster than usual.

Sitting up on the gurney looking forward, his legs covered by a blanket, Paddy answers, "My foot's real ugly, all cut-up."

"But the doc made it better."

"I guess so. Let's go by the clinic and see Ma Gillick. Dr. Strasburg said he's going to take the cast off soon. I want to tell her."

"Nope."

"Then let's go see Miss Minnie for pie or something?"

"Nope."

"Please," Paddy says, turning to him with a make believe pout.

"Ya gotta a surprise come'n."

"A surprise—a good one?" he asks uneasily.

"Yup, a good one."

"Joey's back?"

"No," Johnny Cant answers as he pushes the gurney faster.

The door to the room is completely closed, which it never is. Johnny Cant opens it and pulls the gurney backward into the room. When he swings it around, Paddy can see the outline of a man standing in front of the window. He can't quite make the figure out with the bright sun behind it. He squints—his heart jumps!

"Pop! Pop! Holy cow—wow, it's you!"

"In the flesh." His pop strides up beside him. "Good to see you, son," he says, grasping Paddy's shoulders and squeezing gently.

"Pop, where's Mom and Kate?"

"'Alf-a-mo—say hello to a visitor," he replies, nodding toward the side of the room.

Paddy turns to look. The visitor is coming toward him, his great cap tucked under his arm.

"Uncle Jack!" Paddy cries out with delight.

"Been a while, lad." Uncle Jack places his cap on Paddy's head. "See you still got the *Britannia* sit'n proudly on your nightstand."

"Yes, Mr. Cooney, he's going to let me sail *her* in the pool."

"You must tell me how it goes—if she does indeed float." He chuckles.

"Okay, sure." Paddy smiles broadly, the cap draped over his ears.

"And you got a second visitor as well," his pop says. "This here's Tom Cochran."

A large man with dark curly hair appears from beside the sink. "Hi, Paddy. Nice to meet you." He smiles, coming up to the gurney.

"Hi." Paddy shakes his rough hand which is the size of a baseball glove.

"Mr. Cochran's a carpenter, like your Uncle Jack," says his pop cheerfully.

"You're on a ship, too?" Paddy asks looking up at Mr. Cochran who stands a foot taller than Uncle Jack.

"No," he answers. "Always keep my feet planted firmly set on solid ground. I build houses."

Paddy's pop then turns to Johnny Cant. "We met, didn't we—the day Paddy arrived?"

He responds in almost a whisper, "Yes, sir."

"And your name again?"

"Johnny Cant."

"Aye. Well, this is me Brother Jack, from Liverpool, England. That's Tom beside 'im."

Johnny Cant nods toward the two carpenters and pushes the gurney up to Paddy's bed, quickly lifting him on to it, keeping his legs covered by the blanket. He then props two pillows behind his back.

"See ya." Johnny Cant says placing a third pillow under the heel of the cast. "Ya look good in da hat."

"Bye." Paddy smiles as Johnny Cant goes off with his *clip-clopping* gurney.

"'E's a good chap, son?"

"Yes, really nice," Paddy answers, adding softly as his pop comes up to the bed, "Would you get the Merchant Seaman Pin? It's in the desk top, at the back."

Taking latest *Superman* comic book from the top of the desk, Bill drops it on his son's lap, and opens the desktop while Paddy has his eyes on Uncle Jack who has removed the *Britannia* from the nightstand and showing it to Tom Cochran.

"There you go." Bill attaches the pin to Paddy's gown.

"Why didn't Mom come?"

"She couldn't because ay had to go to New York to see about a job at the Brooklyn Navy Yard." He tosses his overcoat on to Joey's bed. "And your Uncle Jack was in port for a few days, 'is ship docked not far from the Navy Yard. So, ay spent the night onboard. In the morn'n, we met up with Tom Cochran, who was to drive me back to Albany. He got a brother there he'll be visit'n. Your Uncle Jack came along as well—especially to see you."

"Bill," Uncle Jack interrupts, placing the *Britannia* back on its stand, "we'll look around a bit and retrieve the refreshments from the car."

"Aye, but leave the nurses be," Bill laughs.

When they leave, his pop pulls up a chair and sits down beside the bed.

"You're joining the navy, Pop?" Paddy asks he sits down.

"No. Tried. Too old they tell me. I'll be a boilermaker, if ay get the job at the Navy Yard. That's where they refurbish and build ships."

"A boilermaker? What's that?"

"Repair'n ships' boilers. They're tanks, huge kettles— several men at a time can easily stand inside one. They boil the water to make the steam that powers the ship's engines."

"Oh—wish Mom came, too."

"Next time, son. Now, how's the legs?"

"They cut my foot all up."

"Aye, Nurse Kelly said you were off get'n the stitches out."

Bill stands, lifts the covers from Paddy's legs, and looks intently at the cast.

"After Dr. Strasburg took out the stitches, he told me he's going to take the whole cast off soon."

"Aye, now that's good news," his pop answers, lowering the cover then nodding his head toward Joey's bed. "Ay was told you got a roommate, but the bed looks as if it's not being used."

"He's gone."

"Gone? Gone where?"

"Just gone," Paddy mutters. "Maybe he's dead like his cousin Rocco in the iron lung."

"What's this? Your roommate died and this Rocco?"

"I don't want to talk about that. Okay?"

"Aye, as you like."

As Bill sits back in his chair, they hear Uncle Jack and Tom Cochran coming down the hallway chatting and laughing.

"What's that you got there?" Bill calls out with a broad grin as the men enter the room.

"Libations, Bill—covert libations." Tom Cochran laughs, placing a cardboard box filled with opened Coca-Cola bottles on Paddy's desk. "First, served—the young man."

He selects a bottle, sniffs the top, and returns it to the box. He takes another, sniffs that, smiles, and hands it to Paddy. Retrieving three more *coke* bottles, sniffing each, he passes one to Bill, another to Uncle Jack, and keeps one for himself.

"Cheers." Bill lifts his bottle.

Uncle Jack and Tom Cochran raise their bottles. Paddy raises his. And together they take a long drink.

"Nothing like a good swig of *coke*," Tom Cochran says with a satisfied sigh.

"O' aye—and your bit-o-doctor'n don't hurt none either," Bill agrees.

"You got on the lapel pin," Uncle Jack says coming up beside Paddy while Tom Cochran removes his overcoat, places it on the empty bed, and sits beside it lighting a cigarette.

"Yes, it's really nice," Paddy replies.

Uncle Jack picks the comic book up from Paddy's lap and studies the cover for a moment: Superman smashing a Nazi submarine that has torpedoed a ship.

"Good picture—quite real," he says.

"You ever saw a Nazi sub?" Paddy asks.

"Saw one—had the misfortune of be'n sunk by one."

"Wow, you were—were sunk by a Nazi sub?"

"Aye." Uncle Jack drops the comic book back on the bed

"Tell him about it," his pop says. "He'll get a kick out of it, as will Tom. Won't you, Tom?"

"Let's hear it," Tom Cochran answers, slipping the spent match into the cuff of his pants.

"Ready for a good story, lad?" Uncle Jack smiles at Paddy.

"Yes! Yes, please!"

Uncle Jack removes his gold buttoned coat, puts it on Joey's bed, and sits beside it next to Tom Cochran. Placing his drink on the floor, he then takes a black tobacco pouch, a pipe, and a box of wooden matches from the coat pocket. He carefully fills the pipe, sticks the stem between his large brown teeth, removes a match from the box, and with a quick flick of his big thumb nail sets the match alight. Looking kindly at Paddy from under his bushy eyebrows, he sucks the fire into the pipe bole and begins his story.

"Well, it was early even'n, the twelfth of July 1939, and I'm on a 9,500 ton tanker, *The Vancouver City*, sail'n north at eight knots through the St. George's Channel into the Irish Sea. We're carry'n a full load of oil and diesel gasoline from Houston, Texas...only a day out of Liverpool.

"There ay am sit'n on the aft hatch enjoy'n me pipe. Sea calm. Not a cloud in the sky. And quiet, just the low rumbling of the engines and the soft wash of water against the hull. A lovely eve'n it was, 'bout as peaceful as you'd want.

"And I'm feel'n good—blewdy good, indeed—as it was a safe trip. Cross'n the Atlantic in a fully loaded, slow move'n bucket like the *Vancouver* was a highly dangerous business in '39 as the German subs were sink'n our merchant ships faster than we can build them—with an eighty-five percent causality rate, almost as high as the poor blokes man'n the U-boats.

"Well, as ay contently watch a huge sun set'n over the craggy hills of Ireland off in the distance, some'n in the water catches me eye. About two hundred yards off ay'd say. Couldn't quite make it out. So, ay mosey to the rail for a better look. There's some'n all right, and me heart about stopped—a silvery wake cutting through the water and come'n dead on for the ship. Ay cry out at the top of me lungs—Torpedo, to port! Torpedo, to port!—and take off for me fire station like a bat out of 'ell. Before ay'd gone twenty feet there's a thunderous blast, pitching the ship violently and about knock'n me flat on me arse.

"Alarms now blare'n, men race'n about, the bow all smoke and fire, as ay dash on past the galley where to my surprise ay run smack into the galley boy Benny Bryan, a jockey-size lad with a carrot head, freckled face, and bulge'n eyes; thought to be a bit soft in the head.

"There he is empty'n the slop bucket over the side with all hell break'n loose around him. 'Benny!' Ay shout, 'get your blewdy butt to your fire station!'

"And what does the little bugger answer, 'Can't now, sir—ain't done the pots yet!'"

As Bill and Tom Cochran break out laughing, Paddy, too, Uncle Jack takes a long draw on his pipe and then goes on.

"At that moment, ay go blank, and the next thing ay know I'm cough'n up half the Irish Sea with none other than Benny Bryan drag'n up on to a raft. When ay struggle aboard, a bit dazed and feel'n a spud-size lump rise'n above me ear, Benny quickly tells me what happened.

"'As you wuz go'n at me,' he says with a cockeyed grin, 'a second torpedo 'it, toss'n us overboard. Ya must 'uf kissed the *Vancouver's* rail or some'n dur'n our sudden departure. Out like a light ya was when ay got to ya. And as luck would 'ave it, a raft came along wi' us, the blast ay venture break'n it free of its fall.'"

Uncle Jack pauses again to relight his pipe.

"What's a fall?" Tom Cochran asks.

"Ships of the *Vancouver's* class carry several rafts, besides lifeboats." He sucks the match flame into his pipe. "They sit up above the deck on *falls*—skids that let them slide easily from the ship when released."

"What happened next?" Paddy says, wiggling in his bed anxious for the story to go on.

"Aye." Uncle Jack smiles at him, releasing a plume of smoke. "Well, ay get me bearings. The *Vancouver*, she's three hundred yards off, have'n likely gone on a bit after being hit. But now she's dead in the water—clouds of black smoke rise'n from bow to mid-ship. The only movement ay could see on board is lads on the stern, which is still clear, struggle'n to launch a lifeboat—could just make out the orders fly'n back and forth. In the sea between the ship and us are some dozen men, some cling'n to debris, others thrash'n about in the spilt oil...turn'n rapidly into thick sludge by the icy water.

"'Let's go, Benny,' ay say break'n out the paddles. As we pull with all our strength toward our mates, we hear this low brief rumble'n from the ship, not unlike the roll of a kettledrum. Closing in on the lads, the rumble'n comes again, but louder—much louder—followed by an enormous flash throw'n a brilliant white glow over the ship's stern: for a split second highlight'n the lads now frantically lower'n the lifeboat. Then, as if from the bowels of hell, a huge fire ball roars up some fifty feet into the air. The lads, the lifeboat are instantly gone—blown to smithereens."

Uncle Jack pauses, again fiddling with his pipe, while Bill and Tom Cochran sip their *cokes.* Paddy sits wide-eyed.

"With the *Vancouver's* deck now totally ablaze," Uncle Jack continues, "fire suddenly bursts out along her waterline. Feed'n on fuel spill'n from the breached hull, the flame begins spread'n out from the ship like ripples in a pond.

"And we know—we know right away what we 'ad to do as the slick of oil and gasoline is now in the sea around us—save own sorry selves. We quickly swing the raft about and begin paddle'n desperately from the approach'n inferno—and from our hopeless mates. Moving off, we hear the cries of terror behind us as the fire takes its toll."

Uncle Jack pauses and inspects his pipe which has gone out.

"Was blewdy heart break'n, it was," he carries on in almost a whisper while inspecting the pipe. "One of them wretched voices ay heard above the rest was that of me apprentice, Rodney Jackson, only sixteen and his first voyage. Signed on by his dad he was—him think'n the lad safer at sea than in the trenches. A sorry choice that, but who knew it then."

"What's that—an apprentice?" Paddy interrupts softly.

"Someone learn'n to do a job," his pop answers. "The Rodney fellow was work'n under ya Uncle Jack learn'n to become a ship's carpenter."

"Aye, and a good student at that," Uncle Jack says, relighting his pipe. "Well, we get ourselves beyond be'n roasted. The ship about a quarter-mile off—list'n hard to port. She's going down.

"We pull in the paddles, and rock'n easily in the raft we witness the sad sight. The stern goes under first raise'n bow ever so slowly from the sea. And when she's stick'n straight up—a chimney belching black smoke—she hesitates, as if have'n a change of heart. And then with the grind'n and groan'n of metal, the ship slides under. *The Vancouver City* is no more."

Uncle Jack stops again, sucking on his pipe, out again. Bill and Tom Cochran sip their drinks.

"How did you go home?" Paddy asks softly, watching him relight the pipe.

"Ah, Paddy." He glances at him. "I'll get to that, lad. Haven't broke me arm yet."

"You broke your arm?" Paddy says, thrilled there's more to come.

"Aye, that ay did." He smiles. "Should ay carry on?"

"Oh, yes, please," Paddy smiles back at him.

"Now then, no sooner 'ad the ship disappeared into the deep, when Benny, point'n off toward the Irish coast, says quietly, 'Got 'urselves some company, sir.'

"I look towards the green hills, the sun now well behind them, and see the distant outline. It's unmistakable. A blewdy U-boat—and head'n our way."

Uncle Jack sips his *coke*. "It was a frighten'n sight. We 'ad all heard stories, you see, of the U-boats strafe'n survivors. But little we could do but watch, wait, and listen to the dull drone of diesel engines increas'n with the sub steadily approached. We could soon see men at the forward cannon and officers in the conn'n tower, binoculars up take'n stock of their evenings work—and of us. Coming fast, the boat is quickly five hundred yards off, two hundred, seventy-five, close'n in—the men at the cannon gawk'n at us. Us gawk'n back."

"The bow is then above us like a massive mallet ready to strike. Ay shout: 'Benny they mean to ram us to save a shell or two'. Then suddenly, at the last moment, the U-boat veers hard to port, its silver wash fan'n away on the water. Its strikes us a glance'n blow, send'n the raft scrape'n and bang'n up along the gray steel hull. And over we go—the raft flip'n and come'n down on us—all its weight strike'n me arm, plunge'n me under the icy water.

"Gasp'n for air, ay surface look'n up to see the U-boat stream'n by. A hard-faced officer is gaze'n down at me from the conn'n tower—with a bloke beside him take'n pictures of me sorry predicament. Below them, printed in bold white letters is its designation—*U-27*.

"Ay grab the raft, feel'n the sharp pain of me arm, and scan the water for Benny. He's nowhere in sight. Ay work my way around it. Still, no Benny. Then there's a sharp tug on me foot—Jesus Christ—ay screech, think'n for sure I'm to be taken by a shark!

"Thereupon, Benny's red bean pops up beside me. 'Got ya—ay did, didn't ay,' he grins at me as if enjoy'n a summer dip at Blackpool. Oh, did ay want to crack the little bugger one!"

Paddy and the men all laugh and Tom Cochran then rising leisurely from Joey's bed asks, "Another round?"

"Yes, please," Paddy answers, adding hopefully, "Uncle Jack—there's more?"

"O aye," he responds, eyes down checking his pipe.

"Bill?" Tom Cochran offering a *Coke*.

"Aye, wouldn't mind."

"You, Jack?"

"Aye," he says.

Drinks distributed, Uncle Jack returns to his story.

"So, both of us once again in the bitter Irish Sea, Benny scrambles on to the now upside-down raft and again he pulls me to relative safety. By now, the *U-27* is well off toward the edge of night—no doubt in search of further mischief. As the boat fades away, we can just make out an officer on the conn'n tower—swing'n 'is cap as if wave'n good-by! At that, we burst out laughter like a couple of hyenas so pleased we were to still be among the live'n—and we give the *U-27* a one-finger solute in reply."

The men laugh again and sip their drinks while Paddy looks somewhat mystified.

"Uncle Jack," he asks "how do you do a one-finger salute?"

Uncle Jack gives Bill a questioning look.

"Paddy," Tom Cochran jumps in with the answer, "it's like sticking your tongue out at someone, but you flip your middle finger instead—like so."

"Aye, that's it," his pop says, with the men laughing once more.

"Well, to conclude me tale," Uncle Jack takes a pull on his pipe and blowing off a cloud of smoke.

"With the *U-27* out of sight, we settle ourselves down. Ay pull me jacket and shirtsleeve back to inspect me arm. It's thick as a bowl'n pin from wrist to elbow with a nasty red bulge between.

"Pressing the bulge, ay say, 'Benny, it seems broke.'"

"'Oh, aye, don't look like it ain't,' Benny answers in his peculiar manner.

"With that bit of medical wisdom, he curls up on the raft as would a cat on a rug. And ay stretch out, make'n myself comfortable as ay can, me arm now ache'n some'n awful.

"Luckily the night had remained wonderfully clear, the sky brilliant with stars and the moon but a sliver off to the east. Still, it was a cold as a witch's tit and a miserable night with three foot swells roll'n the raft. Don't think ay slept a wink. But at long last, a glow of rose-colored light appears over the horizon. Ay pull myself up to search about other survivors, perhaps a friendly vessel, and hopefully not another marauding U-boat.

"Well, no sooner had ay done so, when a megaphone voice, ghost-like, comes from a bank of fog off to the west: *'Ahoy there! Subs about. Got nets over the side. When we come abreast, jump for it, and scramble aboard.'*

"'Wake up, Benny,' ay yell,' give'n him a good poke with me foot. The craft then appears but a few yards off. 'A ship!' Ay kick him again. 'She'll not stop—we're to jump for the nets.'

"Sit'n up, yawn'n and stretch'n as would a child from a sound sleep, he mumbles, 'Aye, sir—a ship, is it?'

"As the ship approaches, ay gently slide me broke'n wing between me chest and life vest. Benny tightens the vest straps to secure it in place—send'n a stab'n pain through me. It's then alongside us, move'n slowly.

"'Jump, lads! Jump!' the megaphone voice calls. 'It's now or never!'

"With that ay leap to the nets, latch'n on with me good arm. Benny follows, his shoulder push'n up on me arse while holler'n, 'Best get move'n if you would sir! Ya get'n no lighter!'

"There are seamen then in the net on both sides of me shove'n me up and over the gunwale—we 'ad made it!"

Uncle Jack stops. He looks at Paddy with a big, happy grin.

"And now lad," he says "who would you guess is right there to greet me?"

Paddy thinks for a second and then bursts out with glee, "Rodney—your apprentice!"

"Right you are—none other than Rodney Jackson, blackened head to toe with oil but otherwise look'n fit-as-a-fiddle."

"Wow! That's great!" Paddy claps his hands.

"Aye, it was that all right. Lady Luck had smiled on the little rascal—survive'n the hellish fire and the icy the Irish Sea. And Rodney, as ay could plainly see, he's pleased as punch at 'is good fortune. A happy moment for me as well."

Uncle Jack takes his *coke* bottle from the floor and drains it.

"How did he do it?" Paddy asks. "I mean—get away from the fire?"

"Well, be'n a strong swimmer, he swam under the flame'n sludge, so he later told me, and was fortunate enough to reach a lifeboat pull'n from harm's way. It's said that miracles 'happen. Perhaps they do."

"How many survived?" Bill asks.

"Twelve of us survived the *Vancouver*. Two-thirds of the crew were lost, among them the captain and first mate. A sorry reckon'n, that."

"Christ, Jack," says Tom Cochran. "That's quite a story. You read about such things in the papers and see pictures in newsreels. Still, you don't really understand 'til you hear it straight from the horse's mouth. You're a hard man, Jack—getting through all that then shipping out again. Even if I had a mind to go to sea, couldn't do that—never."

"Ahh," Uncle Jack slaps Tom Cochran's thigh. "You could and you would."

"But Uncle Jack weren't you afraid of getting killed?" Paddy asks, still thinking of Rodney Jackson's and how being a good swimmer helped him escape the deadly fire.

"O' aye, so I was." He turns to Paddy. "At sea during war, get'n killed is a real possibility. But it's not being dead that matters as much as how you get there. Ay have never again signed on to a tanker—stay with the freighters. If the sea takes this seaman, the sharks get 'im raw—not fried up like a batch of fish and chips."

Then, the old sailor adds, "Now, lad, every decent story has a lesson or two. No exception here."

Paddy, all ears, looks with anticipation at him.

"First, you never want too quickly to judge'n the full measure of a man—lest you be well off the mark. Ay was mistaken in mock'n Benny, think'n, him soft in the head and all. Ay'd not be here today to tell the tale if it wasn't for him."

Paddy smiles, nodding his head, sipping his Coke.

"Second," Uncle Jack grins, "you want to stay well clear of U-boats and torpedoes unless, of course, Superman is about to save the day."

"Yeah," Paddy beams.

Bill, standing and looking at his wristwatch says, "Well, time we get on our way. The little woman will be wonder'n what's 'appened to us."

Uncle Jack and Tom Cochran get up from Joey's bed, place empty bottles into the cardboard box, and dump cigarette butts from Paddy's drinking glass, *ashtray,* into the wastebasket.

Bill takes Uncle Jack's cap from his son's head. "We're all look'n forward to your come'n home, Paddy—soon."

"I hope so," he responds sadly, glancing toward his cast. "Maybe next time Mom and Kate will come—little Billy, too."

"Aye, we'll see."

Uncle Jack and Tom Cochran come up beside Bill.

"Good luck there, lad." Uncle Jack smiles, reaching out his hand. "See you next trip, God will'n."

"That was really a great story, really great," Paddy says, giving a manly shake and then shaking Tom Cochran's extended baseball mitt.

His pop, smiling a little sadly, ruffles Paddy's hair.

* * *

"Stinks like a brewery in here," Nurse Edelstein says, entering the room waving her hand before her face.

"My pop and Uncle Jack visited me and Mr. Cochran, too," Paddy says excitedly. "And boy, did we have a great time."

Rushing on, Paddy tells her about the torpedoes, the *Vancouver* sinking, the funny man named Benny Bryan saving Uncle Jack, the sailors getting blown up and burnt in oil, the U-boat crashing the raft and breaking Uncle Jack's arm, and how at the end, Rodney Jackson didn't die.

Sitting on the edge of his bed, Nurse Edelstein listens patiently.

"War is terrible, stupid," she sighs when he finishes. "Death and destruction, forever the favorite way of men to solve differences." She then adds with a sharp look, "Paddy, where's your homework?"

"I didn't do it," he says, expecting a scolding.

"Hmm—well okay, this time. We'll take a night off and double up tomorrow. Let's get you into a fresh gown. You can then read your comics for a while and early lights out. You've had a long day."

While Nurse Edelstein finishes helping Paddy into the fresh gown, the words jump out of him.

"Joey's not dead—like Rodney wasn't?"

Paying no attention to his question, Nurse Edelstein says hastily, "I have other work to do. Lights out in ten minutes." She strolls from the room.

Paddy removes his British Merchant Service Pin and stretches over and places it on his nightstand beside the *Britannia*. He settles back under the warm cover and closes his eyes, a smile on his face as Uncle Jack's exciting story plays over in his mind.

CHAPTER XXIII

St. Patrick's Day and "Colombo"
March 17, 1942
Day: Five Hundred and Forty-three

Watching himself moving between the parallel bars toward the mirror, it doesn't look like *real walking*. Dr. Strasburg said it would after he cut off the cast, but swinging the stiff long brace forward, Paddy still sways crookedly to the side—even worse than before the foot was "fixed".

What looks good to him though is his hat. It's a green hat. A "derby hat." That's what Nurse Kelly calls it. She gave him the derby hat for St. Patrick's Day.

"Sure, St. Patrick, he's the greatest Irish saint," she explained, "perhaps the greatest of all of 'em. And yer fortunate to have his name. 'Tis an extra special day for you."

"Okay, Paddy," Ma Gillick calls over to him as he completes lap five, up to the mirror and back. "That's it. We'll finish up. You did very well, very well indeed."

She comes over to him, taking his hand.

"When will Mr. Lombardi make the long brace fixed to bend like before so I can ride my bike again?" he asks as they walk to the exercise table.

"Soon." She boosts him up on it.

"But when?"

"Paddy, soon. Now listen," she smiles unlacing his boots. "I have something to tell you."

"What's that?"

"Well, I'm going to be leaving. I'm going away."

"Where to?" he asks, unbuckling the top strap on the long brace while she does the lower ones.

"To Minneapolis—that's in Minnesota—to join Sister Kenny."

"What? You're going to be a nun?" He looks anxiously at her.

"No—no." She laughs, sliding the long brace from his left leg. "I'm not going to be a nun. And Sister Kenny is not a nun. *Sister* is the title given to nurses in the Australian Army Medical Corps."

"Why are you going?" he mutters. "I don't want you to leave."

She unfastens the short right brace, loosens the boot laces, and pulls it away.

"Why, why are you going?"

Ma Gillick slips off his trousers and socks saying, "I want to learn how to better help children that have polio, like you." She runs her finger gently along the purple scar on top of his left foot which looks irritated. "We'll skip the exercises today and just do the massage and I'll tell you all about it."

"But for how long will you be gone?"

"Well..." she hesitates. "Sister Kenny offered me a job—so, I'll be leaving for good."

"You can't go!" He responds crossly. "It's not fair."

"Paddy." She looks at him, the sides of her mouth turned down into a make-believe frown.

"When do you go?"

"Not for a while. Want me to tell you about Sister Kenny? She is quite an interesting person. "

"No! I don't want to know about her!"

"That's okay. I'll tell you anyway."

Placing her hand on his left knee, she presses down lightly.

Paddy cringes. The bent up leg still doesn't budge, but it hurts less when she tries to straighten it.

"To begin with, Sister Kenny is from Australia. Do you know where that is?"

"No—who cares?" he grumbles, resting back on his elbows.

"Australia is about as far away from here as you can get."

She pushes again on the knee, harder.

"Ouch!" he yells.

"Paddy—*rule two*," she says, not looking at him.

"I don't need your stupid rules anymore. You're leaving."

She ignores his nastiness, which she seldom does. "Now, if you were to dig a hole straight down from here— all the way through the earth—you would come out in Australia, that on the world map looks like a big island."

She reaches for the cocoa butter jar sitting on the end of the table, opens it, scoops out a glob, and begins to rub the cut-up and still *flaccid* foot.

"It's not really an island, though. Australia is a continent—almost as big as the United States. However, unlike the United States, it is mostly a very dry place—the interior, called the *outback*, is desert. So, nearly everyone lives along the coast, except for the sheep ranchers and Aborigines."

"Aborigines?" Paddy asks, showing some interest.

"They're the native people of Australia, like Indians are native people of America. But they don't look like our Indians. Aborigines are dark, mostly very black.

"Like Johnny Cant?"

"Yes."

Paddy flops back hard on the table, toppling the derby hat to the floor, and moans. "I don't want to hear anymore."

"Come on. None of that."

"But do you have to go? Really have to?" He lifts his head.

"Yes. I want to go," she says firmly. "Shall I tell you more?"

"If you have to," he says, wishing she would but whishing she wouldn't, too.

Lying back, he closes his eyes half listing while feeling her hands stroking his feet and legs. She tells how Sister Kenny went into the outback to set broken bones and treat snakebites. How she made children there with polio better using only hot packs and exercise. How she joined the Australian Medical Corps and was shot in the leg—the best part. And how, when the war ended, she went back to helping polio kids again.

"But the doctors in Australia," Ma Gillick finishes, "didn't agree with Sister Kenny's methods. So, she came to America. That was two years ago. Now she has an institute in Minneapolis. And, well, that's where I'm going—to her institute to work with her."

"Don't go." Paddy says, sitting up.

She takes a towel and wipes the cocoa butter from his legs.

"Please." He gently pulls on her sleeve.

"I must." Leaning over, she places her soft hand on his neck and kisses his forehead. "But I'll miss you very much."

"Who cares?" He shoves her away. "I hate this place—and *you.*"

"Now that's rude. Mean! We've been through all that 'I hate' business before."

He falls back, throwing his arm over his eyes. Ma Gillick *puts him back to together*, as she calls returning his legs to their encasements.

"Now, sit up," she says, buckling the last brace strap.

As he rises up, she picks the derby hat from the floor and puts it on his head.

He stares at her, feeling numb with sadness and anger.

"Child..." She places her hands on his shoulders, looking him in the eyes.

"I'm not a *child!*" he shouts.

Heaving a deep sigh, she continues, "Paddy, I must go. You have to try to understand that. I know you're disappointed. Nevertheless, this is one of those times we talked about, when you must be tough inside—the *be tough rule.* Remember, too, you'll be leaving soon as well."

He slaps her hands away. "I don't need you!"

"You ready to go?" Johnny Cant calls from the clinic entrance, wheeling the *chariot* toward them.

* * *

"Sure, you look dead an' dug up," Nurse Kelly says as she makes up his bed. "Cheer up. Eat your lunch. Yer've hardly had a nibble,"

"Ma Gillick, she's going away," Paddy grumbles, gazing out the window from his desk chair: sunny out, but still lots of snow—and no squirrels yet

"So they tell me—off to Minnesota. If yer not goin' to finish yer lunch I'll take the tray."

"The food here always stinks." He shoves at the lunch tray.

As Nurse Kelly removes the lunch tray, Paddy hears a faint *clip-clopping* in the hallway.

He gazes nervously up at Nurse Kelly.

"Johnny Cant's coming back. Am I going somewhere?"

"You would think I know everything?" She shrugs.

The gurney *clip-clops* into the room, a large cardboard box on the front of it. Johnny Cant, flashing his gold-tooth smile, wheels the gurney toward Paddy. Behind the box, he sees something lumpy, covered by a sheet.

"What's all this?" he asks with a nasty tone.

A whispery voice comes from under the lumpy sheet. "Guess who?"

Startled, Paddy looks to Nurse Kelly. She smiles.

The whispery voice again, "I don't wanna stay under here all day. Guess! Guess who!"

"Joey!" Paddy cries out. "It's you!"

The sheet flies away and Joey, grinning ear-to-ear, pops up on his elbows. "Who else?"

"Holy cow! You look different. You got—you got hair," Paddy stutters, hardly believing his eyes.

"Yup." Joey chuckles, sitting all the way up. "Uncle Louie, he cut it when they took the bandage off. Came to the hospital with all his stuff and did it. That was on my ninth birthday. You're still what, five?"

"No. Six. Since December 8th."

Right away, Joey is talking a mile-a-minute in his tough-guy, Brooklyn voice while Johnny Cant pushes him over to the empty bed and lifts him from the gurney on to the bare mattress.

"It's George Raft style. George Raft, he's famous, ya know. Real famous. Plays tough-guys in the movies. There's a picture of him with a boxer on the barbershop wall. He's Tony's favorite actor. Mine, too. What you think?"

He looks at Paddy, running his hand over his black hair which is combed straight back and parted almost in the middle.

"It's real keen—better than the bandage." Paddy laughs, getting up from the desk chair. "But where you been?"

"Mount Sinai."

"Where's that?"

"It's a hospital. It's in Manhattan."

Nurse Kelly puts the uncovered pillow behind Joey and covers his legs with a blanket while Johnny Cant places the cardboard box a chair by the sink.

"You bring your radio?" Paddy asks.

"Sure! Hay, Nurse Kelly," Joey calls out, "get my radio from the box?"

"Later—and the word *please* would help. I'm off now to get sheets an' a pillowcase for you. Be back after a while. Then we'll unpack your things. Now you two," she playfully waves her finger at them, "no shenanigans."

Taking the lunch tray from on top of his desk, she follows Johnny Cant and gurney out the door.

"Gosh, I thought you were dead!" Paddy says walking over to Joey's bed.

"Don't look dead, do I?" Joey grins.

"No." Paddy laughs. "You're the same but with hair."

"Almost was dead, though. Got an infection in my brain from the tube inside." He wiggles himself up against the pillows. "Even got the *Last Rites*."

"What's that?" Paddy says, climbing up on the end of the bed.

"It's when a priest comes and puts oil on ya and says prayers so that ya don't die. But if ya do anyway, every sin you ever committed is forgiven—every single one. And ya go right to Heaven—no Purgatory or anything. A pretty good deal. I didn't die, though." He laughs. *"Close, but no cigar—that's what Tony said."*

"He's still fighting *Nazis,* Tony?" Paddy asks, wondering what dying has to do with a cigar.

"Yup. Couldn't come home even to watch me maybe die. But he sent a letter. That's where he said—*close, but no cigar.* Pretty funny, huh?" He grins and then squinting at Paddy, he asks, "Hay, what's that stupid thing on your head? Looks like an upside down bowl."

"A *derby hat.* And it's not stupid. It's for St. Patrick's Day. That's today."

"I heard of it. Some kind-a Irish big deal?"

"Yeah. Nurse Kelly said St. Patrick is the best saint. He drove all the snakes out of Ireland and turned the heathens into Catholics, too. They're even having a big parade for him, down Fifth Avenue—bigger than any other parade. Even bigger than the Easter Parade."

"Drove the snakes outta Ireland—that's pretty good. Italians, we got Columbus Day for Christopher Columbus. He discovered America. That's a lot better than chasing away some snakes."

"Doesn't have a parade, I bet."

"Ya kidding—a huge one down Fifth Avenue, too— bigger than yours, and one in Brooklyn, too." He pulls himself higher up on the pillows. "Want a funny Columbus poem Tony told me?"

"Okay, but St. Patrick's is the biggest parade."

"Yeah, sure, if ya say so."

Sitting real straight, Joey begins:

In fourteen hundred and ninety-two,
A Dago from It-tally—

"Dago?" Paddy butts in.

"*Dago*—it's what Italians are called. Like you're Irish. So you're a *Mick*. And the Jews, they're *Heebs*. Negros, like that Johnny Cant, are *Niggers*. Japanese, *Japs*. Chinese, *Chinks*. And Germans are *Nazis* or *Krauts*. They're nicknames, but disrespectful."

"Not nice?"

"Yeah, Paddy, mostly. People got 'em, too. Remember Uncle Ralph. The guy I told you who helps Papa collect money. His nickname is *Horse Head Ralph*. That's because of his big head, ugly brown teeth, and long nose—like a horse. No one calls him that, though—not ever. Anyway, not to his face. He'd smash 'em. Like you got to smash anyone who calls you a Mick—or a Gimp."

"I'm a Gimp?"

"Sure, you're a Gimp. That's people with messed-up legs like you and that limpin' guy that brings the food."

"Mr. Martin."

"Yeah, he's one, too."

"What about you—with your messed up legs. You're a Gimp, too?"

Joey shrugs, "Yeah, but I'm more than a gimp. They ain't invented a nickname for me." He chuckles, "Well, not yet anyway. Now, do you wanna hear the Columbus poem—or what?"

"Okay."

Joey starts over:

In fourteen hundred and ninety-two,
A dago from It-tal-y,
Was walking through the streets of Rome,
When he pissed in someone's alley.

"Pissed in someone's alley!" Paddy stops him again. "St. Patrick, he wouldn't ever do that—no way. That's not nice."

"It's not meant to be *nice*. It's funny! Now, don't interrupt! Just listen!"

"Okay."

Joey goes on:

He knew the world was round-o,
He knew it could be found-o,
That masturbating, that castrating,
That son-of-a-bitch Colombo.

"Joey, hold it a second—please."

"You did it again! You interrupted!"

"But how can I think it's funny if I don't know the words? What's masturbating? Castrating?"

"God—ya dumb." He shakes his head. *"Masturbating.* That's what ya do with your *nookie,* your thing, when you get older. It feels all-nice. Tony says it's real fun. And when ya do it long enough, *scum* shoots out, and that's how you make babies."

"What! Joey, that's not true!"

"It is! And *castrating.* Well, under your *nookie* are your balls, the round things in the sack. If they're cut off, ya *castrated."* Joey grins. "Now, that really wouldn't feel too good."

"Columbus, he did that to people?"

"No! No! It's just funny like I said. Listen—okay?"

"Okay."

"So, *Colombo,*" Joey continues:

He goes to Queen Isabella,
To ask for ships and cargo,

And says he'd kiss her royal ass if he could reach
Chicago.
He knew the world was round-o,
He knew it could be found-o,
That masturbating, that castrating,
That son-of-a-bitch Colombo.

Joey stops abruptly, grinning ear to ear. "Good—
ain't it?"

"I guess." Paddy fakes a smile. "But he cut people's
balls off—and there's a parade for him?"

"Hay, it's just a poem, funny remember," he says as
if irritated. "And there's a lot more—even funnier. But I
don't remember it all."

"Can I ask something else now?"

"Sure, shoot."

"How do babies get made out of the *scum* from the
nookie?"

Joey lifts his head, gazing up at the ceiling pipes.
"Well, ya see, girls, they got no *nookies.* And they got no
balls. There's a hole there instead." He pauses, patting
his hair as if to be sure each strand is in place. "And,
well, you put ya *nookie* in the hole. And when the scum
comes, a baby grows inside the hole."

"C'mon," Paddy laughs, shaking his head in disbelief.
"Joey, that's dumb—double-dumb!"

"Well, it's true. Tony, he'll tell you when he gets home
and say the whole poem, too." He turns from the ceiling
pipes and looks at Paddy. "Hay, you know he got shot by
the *krauts.*"

"Tony got shot? Wow! Where?"

"In the arm."

"Uncle Jack, he was torpedoed by a German—*Nazi*—
U-boat. And he got his arm broke."

"You mean the guy that made the *Britannia* was torpedoed—by a sub. Holy shit. What happened?"

* * *

"All right, that's it. Lights out," says Nurse Edelstein. "You two have been at it nonstop. Tomorrow, it's back on schedule. And for you, Paddy, that means getting your homework done."

The lights click off.

Paddy whispers, "Glad you're back, Joey—and not dead."

"Me, too. Mount Sinai stinks. And being dead, I bet that stinks worst." He chuckles.

Paddy takes off the derby hat, places it on his nightstand, and lies back giggling.

"What's so funny?" Joey calls over to him.

"You said, holy shit—*priest poo*."

"I like that." He laughs quietly. "Holy shit—*priest poo*."

Turning on his tummy, Paddy gently rocks his head into the pillow.

"You still do that—that bouncing your head thing?" Joey asks.

"Yeah," he answers sleepily, rocking himself into a dream:

Far below, naked black men are digging in the sand,
Ma Gillick watching them.
Flying down, he shouts out, the words silent:
Ma Gillick! Ma Gillick! Ma Gillick!
Faster—he flies toward her,
His heart thumping—pounding his chest.
Ma Gillick glances up!
Turns away.
She runs from naked black man to naked black man!

They dig faster!
He's getting closer, closer.
The naked black men suddenly stop digging.
They look up, pointing shovels at him,
Their mouths moving:
Gimp! Gimp! Gimp! Gimp!
The sand opens behind them—a big black hole!
They turn quickly away.
They fling their shovels into the hole.
They run, they leap in after them.
The naked black men are gone—disappeared into the darkness.
Ma Gillick runs to the hole.
Looks in.
Looks up at him.
Looks away.
She jumps into the darkness.
Paddy screams:
Ma Gillick!—Ma Gillick!—Ma Gillick!

"Paddy, wake up," Nurse Edelstein is saying softly as he lifts his eye lids. "It's the middle of the night. You're having a bad dream again."

"She's gone," he moans.

"Who? Who's gone?"

"Ma Gillick—jumped into the black hole with the naked black men."

"It's a dream. Everything is fine now. Here, drink this. You're all hot."

Joey groans from the other bed, "Shut-up, will ya? I need my beauty sleep."

Paddy sips the water. The dream is gone.

Chapter XXIV

Sailing the Britannia
April 2, 1942
Day: Five Hundred and Fifty-nine

Last week, Dr. Strasburg released Joey to go swimming. Since then, he has been as happy as Paddy has seen him—and talking non-stop about Brighten Beach, Coney Island, Rockaway Beach, Orchid Beach in the Bronx where his papa's brother lives, and all the other great places he will go swimming with Tony.

Paddy also got some good news as well. Mr. Cooney finally agreed to let him sail the *Britannia*. Even better, he could go with Joey to his first swim session and bring the *Britannia* along at that time.

They're now on their way to the pool in the *vegetable cart.* Paddy is sitting behind Joey who is looking straight ahead clutching *Britannia* balanced between his legs—and, amazingly, he hasn't uttered a word since leaving the room.

"Joey you're scared," Paddy says good-humoredly to break the silence.

"Nah! Ya gotta be kid'n." He answers without turning.

"Bet you are." Paddy chuckles.

"Ah, shut up. If you can swim, I can. That's for sure," Joey answers, his eyes remaining forward.

"You are—you're scared. I can tell."

"I said shut up!" Joey turns sharply to Paddy, almost letting the *Britannia* topple over.

"Cool it, guys—ya all hyped up," Johnny Cant says. "We're almost there."

After maneuvering the *vegetable cart* through the door into the boys dressing room, Johnny Cant announces, "Champ, you first."

He lifts Paddy from the vegetable *cart,* sits him on the changing bench, and helps him remove the braces and his clothes and then slip into the wool swim trunks.

"Now you, Joey." Johnny Cant takes the *Britannia*, sets yacht on the tile floor leaning it against the bench, and he quickly gets Joey undressed.

"It itches," Joey squawks, as Johnny Cant helps him wiggle into the bathing suit.

"Cooties—must-a creeped in ta it." Johnny Cant says teasingly while tying the swim suit drawstring. "The itch'n will stop when ya drown 'em in the water."

"If you don't drown first." Paddy laughs, mimicking Johnny Cant's words the first time he took him to the pool.

"Yeah, real funny," Joey grins.

"Okay, all set." Johnny Cant returns the *Britannia* to its place between Joey's little legs and places towels on the *vegetable cart.* "Hold it tight."

He then pushes Joey through the door and into the sunlight streaming through the pool windows.

"Champ, careful." He looks back at Paddy rising up from the bench. "Ya make it without the braces?"

"Yes—think so," he says uneasily, his legs feeling very shaky.

"Hold a minute. I'll give ya a hand."

Propping open the door with the *vegetable cart*, Johnny Cant takes Paddy's hand and walks with him across the deck to the stairs going down into the water. Grasping the railing, Paddy sits himself on to the top step.

"What do you think, Joey—real nice pool isn't it?" He calls out, sloshing his feet in the warm water.

"Is it warm?" Joey asks, a worried frown on his face, as Johnny Cant wheels him to the stairs.

"Pee-warm." Paddy cups water in his hands throwing it up at him.

"Hey!" Joey giggles. "Cut that out."

Then, coming toward them from far end of the pool, they see Mr. Cooney in his black singlet bathing and carrying a towel.

"Joey," Johnny Cant says, "be back in an hour ta take ya to the clinic. And you, Champ, I'll come for ya after that and get ya back ta ya room."

Then walking toward the locker room he waves at Mr. Cooney. He smiles and waves back while tossing his towel on the bench along the wall.

"Morn'n, lads." Mr. Cooney approaches. "I see ye brought the famoos *Britannia*."

"Can we put her in the water now?" Paddy asks eagerly.

"Later." He comes up beside the *vegetable cart*. "And ye must be me new pupil."

"That's Joey." Paddy smiles. "My best friend I told you about."

"Welcome, Joey. Been swimmin' before, 'ave ye, lad?" Mr. Cooney says, taking the *Britannia* from Joey.

"No, sir," he answers politely, not at all Brooklyn-like.

Holding the yacht at arm's length, Mr. Cooney nods his head in genuine appreciation satisfaction. "'Tis a bonnie ship—fine craftsmanship, indeed."

"Its plank and frame with real sailcloth and brass fittings," Paddy says remembering his pops description.

"O' aye, a work av art. Noo, before the maiden voyage of the gran' *Britannia*, we'll do a wee bit o' swimmin'."

While Mr. Cooney walks over to the bench to place the *Britannia* beside his towel, Joey leans over the side of the *vegetable cart* and says softly, "He sounds like a pirate with that *bonnie, o' aye*—that Long John Silver stuff."

"He's from Scotland. That's the way they talk there. You'll get used to it," Paddy whispers back.

"Paddy, aff ye go," Mr. Cooney says briskly, returning from the bench.

Paddy immediately rolls forward from the step, splashes into the water, and swims underwater across the width of the pool. Surfacing, he looks back to be sure Joey is watching. He is—and with a broad smile.

"Ye regular routine, Paddy," Mr. Cooney's shouts, the words echoing around the pool.

Regular routine, that's ten laps Australian crawl, ten sidestrokes, ten backstrokes, and the water walking. Mr. Cooney still has to help Paddy with the water walking by moving his left leg forward for him on each step. After that, Paddy picks up twenty-five marbles from the bottom of the pool with his right toes—the left ones don't work. Then Mr. Cooney lets him dive for marbles—the most fun.

Paddy stops when he completes the first Australian crawl lap to watch Joey being carried down the pool steps, holding himself tight against Mr. Cooney. *He's scared*; Paddy smiles to himself.

Mr. Cooney shouts to him, "On wi' it. Ye can rest after each set, not before."

Swimming on, Paddy pauses at each end of the pool for a glimpse of Joey, still holding tight to Mr. Cooney who is moving him around in the water. But by the time he stops to rest on his last crawl lap, Joey's on his back, floating easily above Mr. Cooney's out stretched arms.

"Hey, Joey!" Paddy hollers from the far end of the pool, panting a little, "Do-you-like-it?"

"Yeah!" he answers, turning quickly toward Paddy, rolling from Mr. Cooney's arms to sink under the water.

"Paddy! Get movin'," Mr. Cooney barks as he rescues Joey, who comes up coughing and sputtering. Pushing off into his sidestroke laughing, Paddy gags on a mouthful of water and keeps going.

When Paddy finishing his stroke work, Joey is holding the side of the pool practicing dunking under with Mr. Cooney is sitting on the deck above him.

"All right, Paddy, ye can hold up on the rest of ye routine for the day." Mr. Cooney waves him back from the far end of the pool. "Time for the maiden voyage of the gran' *Britannia*."

Going all out, Paddy swims back. When he gets to the pool edge beside Joey, Joey shouts, "Watch!" He then ducks under, pops up, and spews a stream of water into Paddy's face.

As they happily splash each other, Mr. Cooney leans over and lifts Joey from the pool. "'Nough for ye today—ye had a great start, laddie."

He sits Joey on the second pool step, the water just above his waist, and he walks away to get the *Britannia*. Diving under the water, Paddy comes up beside Joey and slide on to the step.

"Here." He hands Joey three marbles

"They're great!" Joey says, carefully inspecting each one.

"You'll be diving for them soon, too. There's hundreds down there."

"Here we go." Mr. Cooney returns to the side of the pool. "The launch of the gran' yacht *Britannia*."

He squats and lowers the shiny brown hull into the water between the boys. Paddy gives the *Britannia* a push.

"Wow, Joey! Isn't that terrific?" he shouts, as the *Britannia* sails swiftly away looking like a true yacht would on a real ocean.

"Could take good ol' *Columbo* ta Chicago, for sure!" Joey laughs as Paddy rolls from the step to swim and dogpaddle after *Britannia*. Catching her, he turns the yacht around and pushes it back to Joey.

After sailing the *Britannia* back and forth between them for a while, Paddy returns to the step. Joey, holding the yacht, stretches his head around watching Mr. Cooney who is now by the bench drying himself.

"Did you ever pee in the pool?" Joey says, turning to Paddy.

"No! You know you can't do that. It's against the rules. Anyway, he'd know for sure. The pee, it'll make the water turn green."

"That's baloney. Won't happen—no way. Let's do it."

"Joey!" Paddy glances over at Mr. Cooney.

Joey shifts the *Britannia* aside with one hand. He then looks down, pointing between his legs with his other hand. A yellow cloud is rising up in the water.

"Joey!" Paddy gasps.

"Do it. Pee." Joey nudges him with his elbow.

Paddy looks again at Mr. Cooney. Turning back, he is still for a moment, watching between his legs. He feels the warm release in his wool trunks as pee drifts up, yellow.

Joey swishes the water. Paddy does the same and the yellow quickly dissipate.

"It didn't turn green," Paddy whispers with relief.

"Told you so," Joey smirks, adding, "Now, what ya say, I tell Mr. Cooney the *Columbo* poem?"

"No, Joey!" Paddy glances nervously toward Mr. Cooney.

"Why not? He'll laugh—think it's funny."

"No. You don't know him! He won't. It's naughty. Please, Joey, don't!" Paddy whispers, panic in his voice.

"I'm gonna."

"No, don't. Don't do it!" Paddy's voice rises.

"Chicken!" Joey says loudly.

"I'm no chicken," Paddy murmurs. "I peed, didn't I?"

"Chicken?" Mr. Cooney is suddenly standing over them. "What ye up tae?"

Joey grins devilishly at Paddy who lowers his head saying to himself: *No, Joey, please don't.*

Joey, smiling brightly, turns up to Mr. Cooney. "Nothing, sir."

"O' aye." Mr. Cooney raises an eyebrow.

Paddy shoves the *Britannia* off toward the far end of the pool, splashes into the water, and races after it.

* * *

After Joey leaves, Paddy and Mr. Cooney, towels draped over their shoulders, sit together on the pool bench for the prayer lesson. Paddy now participates with hidden indifference, partly to please Mr. Cooney but mostly out of being afraid to tell him he doesn't want to do the praying anymore. And just once did Mr. Cooney ask him about the holy medal missing from around his neck. Paddy said he leaves it in his room so it won't get lost in the water.

He lied as well to Nurse Kelly when she inquires about its whereabouts, calming he lost it in the pool.

"Now, Paddy, The Apostle's Creed."

Paddy places his hands together and bows his head, the thought of the Blessed Virgin Mary hanging from the silver chain behind the hissing radiator passing uncomfortably through his mind. Pushing back the guilty thought, he piously recites:

I believe in God, Father Almighty, creator of heaven and earth;

And in Jesus Christ, his only begotten Son, Our Lord:

Who was conceived by the Holy Ghost, born of the Virgin Mary...

CHAPTER XXV

Going Home
May 15, 1942
Day: Six Hundred and Two

"Cigarette?" Dr. Strasburg slides the gold cigarette case across his desk. "And your wife, how is she? She didn't come with you?"

Bill leans forward in his chair accepting the doctor's offer.

"No. The nerves is act'n' up. And there's new baby now."

"Has its ups and downs, M.S. A difficult disease." Dr. Strasburg looks from Bill to a folder before him. "Well now, your son, Paddy, the problem with his ear has been resolved."

"Problem with his ear—what? It's the legs," Bill responds.

"Yes, his legs. But his left ear was infected—*acute inflammation of the middle ear.*" The doctor stops and looks up. "We performed a *myringotomy.* That is, we punctured the eardrum to relieve the internal pressure and inserted a small tube to drain the inner ear."

"Myring…? What the 'ell. When was all this?"

"No one called you?"

"We've no phone," Bill says, searching his vest pockets for matches.

"Well, the ear was operated on, let's see..." Dr. Strasburg returns to the folder. "That was April 2nd Dr. Ingersoll did the surgery."

"Will his 'earing be okay?" Bill asks, lighting up.

"It will be fine. However, he did go through a rough patch that curtailed his physiotherapy progress, the aquatics mainly. Now, let's move on to caring for him when he gets home shall we?"

Bill nods, shifting back in his chair.

"First of all," Dr. Strasburg takes a cigarette from the gold case, "because of the ear problem, he should not submerge his head in water until the tube falls out. That will eventually happen by itself. You do not have to do anything there. Our primary focus of home care is, of course, strengthening your son's legs and improving his balance."

The doctor flicks open a lighter and lights his cigarette, going on, "Paddy must walk as much as he can handle. This is essential. Also, his legs should be massaged daily, putting good downward pressure on the left knee. Hopefully, over time, the left leg will fully extend and gain more length."

"Left's shorter than the right?" Bill leans forward.

"Yes, due to the bend at the knee and some stunting in growth caused by the extended immobilization of the left leg in the long cast. As you recall, both legs were initially in full casts and then the right went to a half cast...."

"Aye, how much shorter?" Bill interrupts.

"An inch or so, right now."

"He'll 'av a limp then, for good?"

"Yes. But when he gets older, you could have his right leg shortened to even the leg lengths."

"What?" Not quite believing his ears, Bill shifts to the edge of his chair. "'Av the right leg, the stronger one, shortened?"

"It's a fairly simple procedure. An appropriate length of bone would be cut from the right femur—the upper leg bone."

Shaking his head, Bill reaches out and crushes his half-smoked cigarette in the gold astray. "Don't know about that."

"Well, that will be your decision," Dr. Strasburg continues. "Now, besides being somewhat shorter, the left leg is also atrophied, withered more so than the right. And it will probably remain that way. However, I must say the incisions on his left foot have mended very well and his gate should improve over time. Still, you must manipulate the foot—up and down, side to side—to try and increase its flexibility as much as possible."

"How's that? Ay thought the foot was fixed."

"The purpose of the operation was to increase stability. This came at a cost...a significant loss of flexibility in the foot. Also, I expect the growth of the foot will be impeded. It will remain smaller than the right foot."

"Christ," Bill mumbles. "Much smaller?"

"Three or four shoe sizes when he is fully grown: a size four or five verses, say, a size eight for the right foot." Indicating an end to the consultation, Dr. Strasburg rocks forward in his chair putting his cigarette out in the ashtray. "Any questions?"

Bill mulls over the inquiry for a moment and then asks, "The braces—what about them?"

"You mean how long he has to rely on braces? You'll have to gauge that. He should soon be able to get along fine without the short one on the right leg."

"Can he walk at all with no braces?"

"Yes, some, unsteadily, according to Miss. Gillick,"

"Aye." Bill nods.

"More questions?" Dr. Strasburg rises.

Hunching forward in his chair, Bill hesitates of a moment and then spits out the words, "Will he always be a cripple?"

"Well, to be honest with you, yes, more or less... depending upon how he progresses at home under your care."

Bill nods again. He takes his overcoat and fedora from the chair beside him and looks plaintively at the battered hat, his face slack with sadness. Then, rising to his feet, he extends his hand across the desk.

"Thank you, doctor, for all you done for the lad."

"You are quite welcome." Dr. Strasburg stands and shakes Bill's hand. "I'll bring the discharge papers to Paddy's room later for your signature."

* * *

Looking out the window from the *chariot,* Paddy calls to Nurse Kelly as she enters the room, "Look, Nurse Kelly! There's snow! On the tree way at the end of the lawn! And it's almost summer!"

"Sure now, that's not snow. 'Tis May—cherry blossom time. Lovely isn't it? A fine day for you all 'round with yer goin' home and all."

"Do I really need to go out in this thing?" Paddy turns the *chariot* from the window.

"You do—'tis *regulation.*"

"Know what Mr. Cooney said the last time I went swimming?" He whirls the *chariot* full circle.

"No, you haven't told me."

"He's going in the army. Like me, everyone is leaving."

"Well, I'm not. Likely be here 'til the devil 'imself comes a knockin'." She laughs and wheels the tricycle from beside the desk toward the *Britannia* which is sitting in its stand by the door.

"You could leave. Be a nurse in the army. Sister Kenny was." Paddy follows her.

"Sure, 'tis not for me." She laughs. "I'll stay put."

"Nurse Edelstein said I could have all the books."

"So you said a ton of times already. I'll pack them— don't you worry."

"And the comics, too?"

"Comics, too."

With a gentle tap on the open door, Dr. Ingersoll walks into the room.

"Hi, Paddy," he says cheerfully.

"Hi." Paddy waves, glad it's not Dr. Strasburg.

Dr. Ingersoll smiles at Nurse Kelly. She responds with a quick curtsey.

"How's the ear?" he asks Paddy.

"Good. Don't hurt anymore. When can I go to swimming again? Joey goes all the time." Paddy pushes the *chariot* up to him.

"A month or so...later in the summer. Let me have a peek at it."

Kneeling on one knee beside the *chariot*, Dr. Ingersoll looks toward Nurse Kelly who is placing books in a cardboard box.

"Obviously no fever, Nurse Kelly. Any nausea, vomiting, diarrhea?"

"No, doctor, nothin' of the kind," she answers coming over to him.

He removes the cotton from Paddy's ear and looks into it using a small light taken from his doctor jacket pocket.

"Seems fine. Like to take a look?" He offers Nurse Kelly the light.

"Oh, indeed." She takes it, squats close beside the doctor, and shines the light in Paddy's ear.

"No sign of *erythematous*—tube seems clear," she says softly, Paddy feeling her warm breath on his cheek.

"You're familiar with the procedure?" Dr. Ingersoll asks with a little surprise in his voice.

"Oh, indeed. You performed a *myringotomy*—a *paracentesis* of the *tympanic membrane* to remove the fluid." She smiles, handing him back the light. "Sure, we learned all that in nursin' school, Dr. Ingersoll."

"Where were you trained?"

"The University College School of Nursing and Midwifery—in Dublin," she says as they both stand.

"I must say, they taught you well."

"Oh, thank you, doctor." She beams, her face glowing red as her hair.

"And how's the walking?" Dr. Ingersoll asks turning again to Paddy.

"Good—real good," he answers.

"Let's have a demonstration."

Paddy rises from the *chariot*. Steadying himself, he then walks to the door and back, stepping strongly with his short-braced right leg while trying hard not to drag left leg and its heavy long brace.

"You're walking quite well now," Dr. Ingersoll complements him.

"Mr. Lombardi fixed the long brace knee so it bends more. Makes it easier—can ride my bike again now, too."

"What about walking without the braces?"

"Not so good," he answers, quickly adding, "but good enough to go home Ma Gillick said."

"When you get home you must walk as much as you can without braces—particularly without the short one. You understand?"

"Okay." Paddy climbs back into the *chariot*.

"When is he to be released?" Dr. Ingersoll addresses Nurse Kelly, who is back packing the moving box.

"This afternoon, doctor."

"Mom and pop are coming to get me," Paddy interrupts, smiling up at Dr. Ingersoll

"How long has he been with us?" he continues addressing Nurse Kelly.

"Nineteen months and a few days, doctor."

"Long time," he replies while squatting beside the *chariot*. He places his hand lightly on Paddy's shoulder. "Well Paddy, I may not be seeing you again. You've been one of my very best patients, and I'm sorry you're leaving. But you are ready to go home—and home you should go. Take care of yourself—and remember, walk, walk, walk."

"Yes, sir, I will."

"Goodbye." The doctor rises to leave.

"Bye." Paddy says, adding with a twinkle in his eye. "You're Santa Clause at the Christmas party."

Doctor Ingersoll gives him a conspiratorial wink and pats his head saying in a hushed tone, "Don't let the cat out of the bag."

He then turns to Nurse Kelly. "Clean the ear out with a little alcohol," he says briskly. "And you had better repack it as a precaution."

"Yes, doctor," she answers smartly.

Then following Dr. Ingersoll out the door, Nurse Kelly looks back at Paddy. "I'll be gettin' another box. You may want to start by emptin' your desk while I'm gone."

"I will," he says and adds loudly, "Dr. Ingersoll's the best doctor—not fake-y like Dr. Strasburg."

She brings her finger to her lips, shaking her head, shushing him.

When they disappear into the hallway, Paddy pushes the *chariot* to his desk, slides away the desk chair, and sits staring out the window hoping to see the squirrels. They were running up and down the big tree all morning, two big ones and two little ones.

"Sure, in all the commotion didn't I almost forget." Nurse Kelly comes rushing back into the room. "You got a postcard!"

"A postcard! From who—who'd send me one?" Paddy turns the *chariot* from the window.

"Who else—Ma Gillick. An' all the way from Minnesota."

"Wow! Let's see!"

She hands him the card. He studies it for a moment, a picture of a large building with words under it on the front, and turns it over looking at the writing thinking: *nice and neat letters like Pop's.*

"You read it." Paddy holds the card up to Nurse Kelly.

"Sure, read it yerself. Don't be so lazy."

"Please. It'll sound better if you do it."

"Well, I shouldn't. Nurse Edelstein would have me hide. But 'tis your last day—can't spoil you too much more now can I."

She takes the card and sits beside him in the way too small for her desk chair.

"Well, let's see. Under the grand lookin' buildin', it says *Northrop Memorial Auditorium.* Below that, *University of Minnesota.*"

"Read what Ma Gillick says," he says impatiently.

Turning the card, she clears her throat. "Ready?"

"Yes!"

Dear Paddy:

I am all settled in here at the Institute. We have a fine clinic, large and well equipped. And Sister Kenny is very nice but strict—not so soft like me! I know you are working hard—and remembering the rules—and should be going home. I do miss you. Say hi to Nurse Kelly for me.

Love,
Ma Gillick
XXXOOO

Nurse Kelly then turns the postcard over to look at the picture again, saying, "That buildin' looks much like where I had classes at University College—all the columns and ...."

Paddy grabs the card from her hand. "That's all she said?"

"Yes. And a lovely card, 'tis." She rises from the desk chair. "Now, let me repack your ear before I forget that as well."

While Paddy is studying the card, flipping it front and back, and Nurse Kelly presses cotton into his ear, the gurney *clip-clops* into the room returning Joey from swimming.

"Hay, know what?" Joey shouts. "He's going in the Navy!"

"Who?" Paddy slips the postcard into the desk.

"Him—he is." Joey points back over his shoulder at Johnny Cant.

"*You*—you're going in the Navy?" Paddy watches Johnny Cant roll the gurney up beside Joey's bed.

"Right, *Champ!* Uncle Sam's gonna teach me ta be a cook—like Miss Minnie." He lifts Joey on to his bed. "A darn sight better then lug'n a Brooklyn Dodger fan around."

"Wow—when?"

"In three weeks."

"Oh," Paddy says quietly, somehow feeling sad that everyone is leaving even though be soon gone as well.

"Now, empty your desk, Paddy," Nurse Kelly orders, having finished packing his ear. "An' put it in that paper bag I gave you."

"Okay."

She and Johnny Cant depart, Joey, combing back his George Raft cut, is quietly flip through the *Sporting News Record Book* while. Paddy moves the *chariot* up to the desk, opens the top, and begins taking out items and placing them on his bed:

* Ma Gillick's postcard,
* British Merchant Service Pin,
* Red and silver horseshoe magnet wrapped with string,
* Latest *Superman* comic,
* Fountain pen and bottle of blue ink,
* Box of *Crayolas*,
* Hubley Cap Pistol.

When finished, Paddy maneuvers the *chariot* around the side of the desk, He glances at Joey who is now engrossed in reading one great record of another, and then leans way forward in the seat to look up behind the radiator, turned off now and not hissing now. He sees it. The holy medal is high up hanging from a rod securing the radiator to the wall.

"Hay! What ya doing?"

Startled, Paddy throws himself back in the chariot answering, "Looking for the squirrels."

"And what you doing in *my chariot?*" Joey snaps shut the *Sporting News Record Book.*

"They have to take me out in it. Besides, it's not *yours.*" Paddy moves back behind his desk.

"Let's see the pistol, Paddy."

"That's mine—I want it back." He tosses it on to Joey's bed.

"For sure, thanks."

Picking up pistol, Joey aims it at the doorway where Mr. Martin is just limping into the room, a lunch tray balanced in each hand above his head.

"Food!" He says with his gummy grin.

"What ya got?" Joey pulls the pistol trigger—*click, click, click.* "I'm starving."

"So, what else is new?" Mr. Martin says, handing Joey his tray.

"Yuck," Joey wrinkles his nose, "hot dogs and them beans—the musical fruit, the more ya eat the more ya toot. Why never no pizza?"

"Miss Minnie don't do pizza."

"That ain't right." Joey fires the cap gun at him—*click, click, click.*

Taking no notice, Mr. Martin places Paddy's tray on the desktop before him, asking, "Ya leav'n, kiddo?"

"Yeah. This afternoon," Paddy answers looking at the watery beans.

"Remember the poem I taught ya—when ya first got here?"

"Sure," he answers and quickly rattles it off without taking his eyes from his lunch:

Thirty days has September,
April, June and no wonder,
All the rest eat peanut butter,
'Cept grandma,
She rides a tricycle.

"Hey, I like that," Joey laughs as he carefully prods his hotdog with a fork. "How come you didn't tell me it?"

"Forgot."

"That wuz good," Mr. Martin says, "I now got a go'n home one for ya. Wanna hear it?"

"Yeah," Joey answers, munching the hotdog.

Paddy nods, scooping up some beans.

"Okay, here goes."

They stop eating, their eyes on Mr. Martin. He limps to the center of the room, faces them, then swaying easily from side to side, like a branch caught in a breeze, he singsongs:

Mama, mama take me home,
From this reconstruction home,
I've been here a year or two,
Now I want to go home with you.
Ta rah rah boom de ay,
Ta rah rah boom de ay,
Ta rah rah boom de ay,
Ta—rah—rah—boom—de—ay!

Mr. Martin stops swaying and gives the boys his big gummy smile like that's his best creation yet.

"That's great!" Paddy claps.

"Do it again," Joey mumbles, stuffing his mouth with the *musical fruit.*

"All right. Then ya turn," Mr. Martin says.

He singsongs again. And when he finishes, Joey and Paddy looking gleefully at each other shout:

Mama, mama take me home
From this reconstruction home,
I've been here a year or two,
Now I want to go home with you.

And then they howl at the top of our lungs:

Ta rah rah boom de ay!
Ta rah rah boom de ay!
Ta rah rah boom de ay!
Ta—rah—rah—boom—de—ay!

"What's the racket?" Nurse Kelly enters the room carrying a cardboard box.

"A going home song—Mr. Martin taught us," Paddy says, laughing along with Mr. Martin and Joey. "Want to hear it?"

"Haven't I already—an' all the way down at Times Square." She drops the box inside the doorway.

Mr. Martin, turning to go says to Paddy, "If ya gone before I'm back for the tray, take care kid-o—and don't take no wooden nickels."

"Bye." Paddy waves as he hobbles out the door. He then calls to Nurse Kelly, who is leaving behind Mr. Martin, "Do me a favor?"

"What?" She stops.

Casting a brief look at Joey, who is occupied with the cap pistol and his food, Paddy motions for her to come to him.

She walks up beside the desk. He waves her closer. She squats down.

"My holy medal is hanging behind the radiator," he whispers.

"What? Your holy medal? Now, how in the name of God did it get there?" She says softly, looking up at the dormant radiator.

"I can't tell you." He whispers once more.

"And why not?" Again softly.

"I don't want to. Please, can you just get it for me—and without Joey seeing?"

"Humm." She frowns at him.

Nurse Kelly then stands and steps over to the window, as if looking out. She glances at Joey, fiddling with the cap pistol, and reaches up behind the radiator.

She returns and squats back down beside Paddy. "Here you are. Now, you must tell me how it got way up there behind the radiator."

"No," he mutters shaking his head and taking the holy medal.

"You should tell me. I retrieved it for you."

"No. Please don't ask anymore, okay?"

"Ah well, as you like. I guess a holy metal flyin' aff and hidin' itself behind a radiator will remain one of the world's grand mysteries." She rises and takes the paper bag from Paddy's bed and hands it to him. "Now, eat up and then finish packing-up."

"Thanks for getting it." He smiles, dropping the holy medal in the bag.

"Now, you two." Nurse Kelly goes to the door while looking at Joey. He glances up at her. "Keep the noise down to a low roar. I'll return after lunch."

Joey puts the cap pistol aside when Nurse Kelly leaves and starts talking away while gobbling up his lunch.

"The Dodgers are gonna take it all this year, you know Paddy. Johnny Cant doesn't think so, but what does he know. With Camilli, Walker, and Medwick providing the hitting power—we're unbeatable. An' Pee Wee Reese, he'll be MVP again. That's for sure. But Durocher, he could fuck it all up—like last year. Don't know his ass from his elbow 'bout managing, Tony says."

"Ass from his elbow." Paddy laughs, chewing the last of his hotdog.

"Yeah! That's good, ain't it?" Joey mumbles with half a hot dog in his mouth. "Tony, he says that all the time or—'he don't know shit from shine-o-la'."

"Shine-o-la?"

"Shoe polish! You jerk!" Joey looks at him, adding, "Give me a few of your comics. You don't need to take them all."

"Oh, okay."

* * *

The cheerful voice comes from the doorway. "Aye, Paddy—ready to go?"

"Pop!" Paddy spins the chariot from the desk.

Bill strolls into the room, followed by Nurse Kelly. He comes up alongside his son and drops a paper bag on to the desk top while tossing his fedora on the bed.

"What you do'n in that thing?" he says, looking at the *chariot.*

"I have to be wheeled out, Pop—it's regulation. What's in the bag?"

"New clothes your mum sent."

"Where is she?" Paddy looks past him to the door.

"She stayed home to take care of little Billy. You'll be see'n your mam in no time."

"Oh," he sighs. "Wish she came."

"What's your name, lad?" Bill looks over at Joey.

"That's Joey," Paddy answers as he pulls the new clothes from the paper bag.

"Joey, the roommate you told me about last time?" With a puzzled look, he turns back to his son.

"He's not dead, Pop." Paddy laughs.

"Aye, that's plain to see," he says going to Joey and extending his hand. "Glad to meet you, lad."

"Hi." Joey shyly shakes the hand.

"When can we go, Pop?" Paddy as he lays the new clothes out on his bed.

"We have to wait a bit for Dr. Strasburg," his pop replies, fixing his eyes now on his Paddy's legs. "The doctor said you could walk without them braces."

"I can, some."

"O' aye. We'll leave 'em then."

"Leave the braces?" Paddy mutters, looking worriedly toward Nurse Kelly who is by the door finishing packing his comics.

Turning and smiling nicely, she says, "Maybe we should ask Dr. Strasburg about that."

"Aye," Bill grumbles. "But they must come off to put on his new clothes. Can you give the lad a hand?"

"Indeed," she says, closing the top of the comic book box.

"And how are you get'n along?" Bill turns his attention back to Joey.

"Good. I go swimming now. Just got back."

"Bet ya a good swimmer."

"I'm getting real good. But not like Paddy—not yet, anyway. He's a shark." Joey grins at Paddy who grins back.

"So I'm told," Bill replies, a touch of doubt in his voice.

"And Pop, we sailed the *Britannia* in the pool," Paddy says as Nurse Kelly helps him out of his braces.

"'Ow she go?"

"Great! Just push a little and it, *she,* sails way to the end of the pool and then..."

"Hello there," a familiar voice cuts Paddy short.

Nurse Kelly stands and curtseys. Joey waves casually.

"Hello Dr. Strasburg," says to Bill. The doctor nods to him in reply.

Paddy grunts, "Hi."

Joey says nothing, dropping his eyes to the cap pistol in his hand.

"Well, today's the big day, Paddy?" The doctor comes up beside the *chariot.*

"Can I walk out?" Paddy asks hurriedly. "Nurse Kelly says I'm not allowed to."

"We can probably bend the rules a little."

"That means ya don't take *my chariot*?" Joey calls from his bed.

"Right—it's yours, now—all yours." Paddy smiles at him.

"Good," he says, aiming the cap pistol around the room as if scouting out a likely target. He pauses with Dr. Strasburg in his sights uttering quietly, "pow, pow."

"My pop wants me to leave them, the braces," Paddy says to Dr. Strasburg, as Nurse Kelly, squatting in front of the *chariot,* slides off his long brace.

"Aye," Bill says. "He should be get'n along on his own now like you said, doctor."

"He must do that," Nurse Kelly interjects politely. "But taking the braces and usin' them a while longer will do no harm an' help him to get around more easily. He's not quite ready to..."

"No harm?" Bill says looking sharply at her. "He'll draw enough attention to them polio legs without the braces."

"Not necessarily so, an' besides..." Nurse Kelly counters.

"Yes, well," Dr. Strasburg jumps in addressing Bill, "we'll leave the braces off, but take them with you."

"All right with you, son?" Bill turns back to Paddy.

"Sure," he answers, looking at Nurse Kelly rolling her eyes to heaven as she removes the short brace.

She places it on Paddy's bed beside the long brace and begins helping him into his new clothes while Dr. Strasburg and Bill step away to go over some papers.

"I'll have no shoes—they're attached to the braces," Paddy says quietly to her.

"Yes," she says sharply. "Yer'ill walk out in yer hospital slippers as yer father wants."

Bill turns from Dr. Strasburg. "I'll get him some shoes soon as we get home."

"That'll be grand," Nurse Kelly responds, adding under her breath, "*shoite!*"

Without braces and dressed in his new clothes—white shirt, blue jacket, brown corduroy knickers, brown knee-high socks, and blue hospital slippers—Paddy rises from the *chariot* and walk shakily to Joey's bedside.

"Ya look cool—like then blue slippers. A nice touch," Joey says with a chuckle.

"Thanks." Paddy bends over and pulls up the left leg of knickers. It has slid down his calf, which is stick-like compared to the more muscled right leg.

"You'll visit me in Brooklyn, right?" Joey asks. "We'll hang out. Watch the *bocce* guys. Listen to baseball—maybe see a stickball fight. And Uncle Louie, he'll give you a George Raft cut. Go good with the new duds,"

Joey then grins and slicks back his hair with his palm, adding. "Now, how about the comics ya gonna give me?"

"All right," Paddy smiles.

He makes his way to the cardboard box containing the comics, select six, totters back, and hands them to Joey. Flipping hurriedly through them, he removes three *Red Ryder* comics.

"I'll trade you these *Red Riders* for three more *Superman.*"

"What! They're my comics! You can't trade like that."

"You gave 'em to me. They're mine." He holds out the three *Red Ryders.*

"Yes, but..."

"I own 'em now. I can trade 'em," Joey insists.

"Okay. But it's not right," Paddy says with a half smile and heads back to the cardboard box.

"What about these *Red Ryders?* You want 'em, or what?" Joey asks.

"Nah. You can have them—read them a hundred times."

When he returns with two more *Superman* comics, Joey grabs them saying, "Hay—that's all? Ya stiff'n me. There are three *Red Ryders.*"

"Joey—c'mon! That's not right, not fair," Paddy objects angrily. "You're keeping the *Red Ryders.*"

Joey laughs saying, "Can't blame me for trying. Here, don't be mad—a going home present." He fishes under his pillow and hands Paddy a rolled-up newspaper tied with string. "Don't open it now—later."

"What is it?"

"You'll see."

"Paddy, we're off," his pop says, donning his fedora.

"Good luck, Paddy," Dr. Strasburg calls out as he is leaving the room.

Paddy ignores the doctor saying to Joey, "Have to go—see you."

"Not if I see you first," Joey replies, turning his attention to a *Superman* comic.

Paddy turns away and wobbles over to his pop. He takes his son's hand, saying to Joey, "Take care, lad."

"Sure," Joey answers, not looking up from the comic book.

Nurse Kelly removes the braces from the bed and places them on the gurney where Johnny Cant has put the tricycle, the *Britannia* and stand, and the cardboard box with all Paddy's possessions, the *Red Ryder Pop Gun* sticking from the top.

At the door, Paddy stops and looks back for the last time at the room: his neatly made bed; his nightstand, gloomy without the *H.M. Cutter Yacht Britannia* resting majestically on top of it; the silver radiator above the nightstand, not hissing now; the bare window and big tree outside, a squirrel frozen on the trunk gazing back at him; the chair and the desk below the window, the slanting desk bright in the sunlight; Joey's nightstand and his bed, where he sits intently reading a comic book; the two green chairs by the sink; the *chariot*, looking somehow lost in the middle of the room: and the red brick walls—"Like some 'ol basement storage room," his mom's words popping into Paddy's mind.

"Bye, Joey," he calls out, feeling a pang of sadness at leaving his best friend, the room they shared, and their happy times together.

"Yeah," Joey grumbles, gracing up from his comic book.

Paddy and his pop then follow Nurse Kelly, Johnny Cant, and the *clip-clopping* gurney out the door. They turn down *Thruway*, Paddy looking out the arched windows at the long tree shadows stretching across the field. Suddenly a blast:

BANG!

Then, again in quick succession:

BANG! BANG! BANG!

Startled, they stop abruptly and look back down the hallway.

"What's that?" Bill asks.

"My cap pistol." Paddy answers, his heart racing with delight. .

"Be-jays us! The little devil," Nurse Kelly glairs down at him. "An' where did he get the caps? He said he gave me all of 'me."

"I don't know." Paddy shrugs, unable to restrain a big grin.

"Oh, I'm sure you don't. I'll go get your gun."

"No, he can have it."

"You sure?" She asks.

"Yup, it's Joey's now."

Nurse Kelly looks at Paddy for a moment longer and then heaves a sigh. "Well, 'tis yours to give."

Moving on towards Times Square, the caps blast away yet again:

BANG! BANG! BANG!

"Agh! The rascal!" Nurse Kelly gasps as they all stop once more. "He'll be the death of me yet. I must go back."

Crouching down beside Paddy, she says softly, "I best be leavin' you here."

"Please come out all the way with me?" he sighs.

"I must go back." She hugs him gently.

Letting go of his pop's hand, Paddy throws his arms around her neck, squeezing with all his might as if to pull here inside side him so she could never leave.

"May God bless you love," she says tenderly, her cheek pressed against his, "but you don't want to be stranglin' me, do you?"

He takes a big gulp of air, not wanting to cry like a baby. "Sorry," he says softly while releasing his grip some but still holding tight.

"I'll always remember you, love," she whispers softly, her eyes glistening with tears.

She gently untwines Paddy's arms from around her neck. Then, pulling the left knickers pant leg up into position, saying, "Your mother can use a rubber band to keep this side from slidin' down."

Giving his cheek a quick peck, she stands, turns briskly, and trots back toward Joey and the cap pistol.

* * *

"Well, Champ, this is it. Ya go home. I go in the Navy," Johnny Cant says, looking down at Paddy holding on to the gurney watching his pop trot off to get the car.

Paddy looks up. "You know, Joey's my best friend, and you're my best friend, too."

"I take that as a compliment." He laughs quietly.

They then wait in silence. A white car soon pulls up beside them. Bill jumps out. He rushes to the back of the car and opens the trunk. Johnny Cant takes the cardboard box from the gurney and places it inside. Bill slams the trunk shut, opens the rear door of the car, gets the tricycle from the gurney, and wiggles the bike into the back seat. Johnny Cant then carefully places the *Britannia* beside it.

"The braces?" Johnny Cant asks, returning to the gurney.

Bill glances at Paddy for a moment as if deciding to leave them then says, "Better give 'em here."

Taking the braces, he tosses them onto the floor in front of the back seat and closes the rear door.

Opening the passenger side door, he turns to his son. "Well, lad, let's go—'op-in.'"

Paddy releases the gurney, totters to the car and slides butt first into the seat, his left leg dragging as he tries to turn into position.

"Here, I'll help with the bum *leg*," his pop says while bending down to assist him.

"No, I got it, Pop." Paddy pivots around and pulls the leg into the car, thinking with a smile: *Bum Leg—the dumb thing got a nickname. Joey, he'd like that.*

"A little some'n for your trouble," Bill says, extending a five dollar bill to Johnny Cant.

"That boy's been no trouble, sir, none." Johnny Cant raises his hands, rejecting "the little some'n".

"Aye," Bill replies. "Thank you. He's a good lad."

"So long." Paddy waves to Johnny Cant.

His pop closes the door and rushes around the front of the car, opens the driver's side door, and hops into the car.

"Take care, *Champ*." Johnny Cant gives Paddy a big gold tooth smile as the door bangs shut.

Driving off, Paddy looks back watching the black giant pushing his *clip-clopping* gurney leisurely toward the hospital entrance.

He waves and then turns to his pop. "Where did you get the car? It's nice."

"Belongs to the college." His pop looks over at him. "How you do'n?"

"Great," he replies.

As the car swings around the hospital building, Paddy watches out the window. He sees what looks like his big tree and the window to his room. He giggles to himself, thinking: *Joey's getting the dickens from Nurse Kelly right now—she won't get all the caps, though. That's for sure*

"Want the radio?" Bill asks as they start down a long winding hill.

Paddy turns from the window. "It's got a radio, wow. Can we put on the five o'clock stories?"

"Five o'clock stories?" His pop glances at him.

"Me and Joey, we listen to them all the time."

"Aye, but it's only about four. We'll 'ear the news for a bit first."

He clicks on the radio:

The last Japanese were evacuated from San Francisco. Six Greyhound buses carried 274 from the collection point at Raphael Weill School to the Tanforan assembly center. Only six seriously ill Japanese remained in local hospitals.

Paddy unties the string from Joey's package and unfolds the newspaper across his legs. Lying side by side are three led soldiers. One standing firing a rifle. Another down on one knee shooting. The third at attention, a rifle over his shoulder. Smiling, he rolls the soldiers back up in the newspaper and reties the string.

The Navy has seized an entire San Francisco neighborhood to add to the Hunters Point base facilities. About 100 families will be forced to move for what the Navy called military necessity. This includes the elderly parents of baseball star Joe DiMaggio.

"He plays center field for the *Yankees*." Paddy says, looking over at his pop.

"Who's that?" He glances back.

"Joe DiMaggio. The baseball star the radio is talking about."

"How you know he plays for the Yankees?"

"Joey, he told me. He knows all about baseball—like Joe DiMaggio had a fifty-six-consecutive-game-hitting streak last year. But we're for the Brooklyn Dodgers. Pee Wee Reese is our favorite player. Who do you like? Dodgers or Yankees?"

"If you're a Dodgers fan, I'm that as well." His pop smiles. "Besides, I'll soon be work'n at the Navy Yard. That's in Brooklyn. We'll be move'n from Albany."

"To Brooklyn—that's where Joey lives," Paddy says, turning excitedly to his pop.

"No, we're go'n to live in Queens, Astoria."

"When?" he asks, disappointed it's not Brooklyn.

"Couple-a-weeks."

"Is that far from Brooklyn?"

"Astoria, not far."

At the bottom of the hill, the car stops. Paddy looks out the car window. Planted in the grass is blue sign with white letters:

NEW YORK STATE
RECONSTRUCTION HOME
EXIT ONLY

ABOUT THE AUTHOR

Patrick J. Bird was born and raised in New York City. He has degrees from the University of Illinois, B.S. and M.S., and the University of Minnesota, Ph.D. He has held professorial and academic administrator positions at the University of Minnesota, University of Virginia, and University of Florida and was gymnastics coach at the University of Illinois and the University of Minnesota in the early part of his career.

He has published articles in popular magazines including *Scientific American* (online), *Women's Health, Cooking Light, Your Family* (Florida), and *Golden Years*. For thirteen years, he wrote a weekly health column for the *New York Times Regional Newspaper Group* and the *St. Petersburg Times* and has fifty plus academic publications to his credit.

Pat is married and has three grown children. Retired from academia, he lives and writes in Gainesville, Florida.